Gran's Old-Fashioned C

GRAN'S OLD-FASHIONED GARDENING GEMS

by Jean Penny

(author of *Gran's Old-Fashioned Remedies, Wrinkles and Recipes*)

EX LIBRIS PRESS

First published in 1992
Reprinted in 1993
Reprinted in 1995 by

EX LIBRIS PRESS
1 The Shambles
Bradford on Avon
Wiltshire

Typeset in 10 point Century Schoolbook
Design and Typesetting by ExLibris Press
Cover by 46 Design, Bradford on Avon

Cover printed by Shires Press, Trowbridge
Printed and bound in Great Britain by
Cromwell Press Ltd., Broughton Gifford, Wiltshire

ISBN 0 948578 35 1

*To a great gardener,
and the best friend I could have wished for:
My Mum*

Acknowledgement: The publisher wishes to thank
M'lou Lewellyn of Douch Farm Nurseries,
Bradford on Avon, for her assistance
with the illustrations in this book.

CONTENTS

Preface

'Old-fashioned', because some of the tips come from my grand-mother's days and beyond. 'Old-fashioned', because some of my own gardening experiences caused me to use some rather old-fashioned words.

Perhaps I should say straightaway that, by the time I had acquired a house and garden of my own, I was not a complete stranger to gardening. Had I not, as a child, planted seeds in 'my very own garden'? The fact that my seeds, unlike my brother's and sister's, never grew up to face the world gave me little encourage-ment. By the time I was ten years old I was fairly convinced that I did not have green fingers: more like black thumbs.

Later, as the only offspring remaining at home, I tried, during periods of family sickness, to keep the garden in order. It was from my mother that I learned to appreciate gardens and gardening.She had many talents, not least of which was her gift for gardening. My Mum brought to gardening, as she brought to everything she tackled, an abundance of love and enthusiastic interest. She fairly flung herself into gardening with an energy which I found ex-hausting to witness! But gardens flourished under her care. She used the 'old ways' and time, not money. And she reaped what she sowed.

When the time came for me to become a garden owner I tackled my ground with some experience, little confidence but unexpected interest. I was not as thorough as I could have been; my mistakes, muddles and acquired knowledge, which included the 'old ways' (for I do not subscribe to spending too much time or money on my garden) are spread over the following pages for your assistance, enlightenment and comfort.

Jean Penny
Somerset, 1992

1 A BLOODY-MINDED BUSINESS

What a man needs in gardening is a cast-iron back with a hinge in it.

Charles Dudley Warner

The most important thing to remember about gardening is that there is no beginning and no end to the gardener's working calendar: it goes on forever. This is daunting knowledge.

Another observation to demoralise you is that time, or rather lack of it, is constantly dogging the gardener. This is not to mention the weather — even the seasons will conspire to muddle your plans — and the difficulties, nay the obstinacies, of the soil. All in all gardening is a bloody-minded business.

Some irritatingly tidy folk will somehow contrive to make a flower garden out of a tiny town patch, complete with minute, handkerchief-size lawns — a smooth green lawn on which every blade of grass appears to have been regimented into position. I once knew an ex-Army chap who seemed to get all his plants and flowers to stand to attention regardless of the weather. I expect it was all the drilling. There are some with much larger sites who seem to achieve enviable results. I daresay some of these garden owners employ gardeners.

Whether you take over a mature garden (and don't forget that mature can mean that everything is just about played out, or that it is about to reach that state) or take over virgin ground, you will need a plan. Always plan — indeed, the planning can be great fun. It is the carrying out of the plans that is none too funny.

There are those who will tell you that it can be very rewarding to achieve order out of another's chaos. There are others who tell you that it can be exciting to acquire a garden which has been unplanted and in which you can arrange the entire garden entirely to your own satisfaction. Which only goes to show that some people will say anything.

Although there is no beginning and no end to the gardener's calendar, it is necessary to begin somewhere. However, if you are taking over another's garden, I would advise waiting a year (oh the bliss!) before rooting anything out, unless a tree is about to descend on to your roof, or the honeysuckle is on the rampage. Of course, you will still have to weed the garden, and mow the lawn, and also dig out the vegetable garden. But if you have the courage to do so, be idle and wait and see what comes up. Make a note of the appearances during the year and then plan your garden accordingly (alternatively, move to a high-rise flat).

SOME GARDENING TERMS

ANNUALS
Plants which live for one season only. Clarkia, petunia, sunflower, cornflower, love-in-a mist, sweet pea, poppy, nasturtium — these are all annuals. Annuals means you have to plant them every year. Very depressing. I do not entertain annuals in my garden, though I do enjoy them in other people's gardens. (Note: just to confuse you straightaway — some poppies are perennials, I have some in my garden).

BIENNIELS
Nearly as bad as annuals because they only last two years and often you sow them one year to flower the next. That is to say, some of them grow the first season and produce flowers the second. Wallflowers, honesty, sweet william are some biennials. It is a pity for me that sweet william is a biennial for I really would like to have it in my garden. However, I have only sufficient time for the good old perennials.

COMPOST
A manure made from decayed animal and vegetable refuse and sometimes mixed with lime. Coarse sand is useful for mixing in compost, particularly in compost for the growth of pot plants, because it helps to carry off the excess of moisture from the roots.

DECIDUOUS
Trees and bushes which shed their leaves in one season.

EARTHING-UP
Drawing the earth up to the stems of plants in a row and so forming a ridge.

EVERGREEN
Trees and bushes which keep their foliage through the winter.

GRAFTING
Uniting a shoot of one plant to the root or branch of another.

HALF HARDY
Describes those plants which should be wintered under glass in frost-free conditions.

HARDY
Plants which should withstand most British winters (but don't blame me if we get an Arctic winter).

HERBACEOUS
Plants which die right down to the root every year.

LEAF MOULD
Garden mould into which has been mixed a heavy proportion of decayed leaves. Annuals respond happily to leaf mould.

MULCH
Materials used for preserving moisture around and about the roots of plants. This can be farmyard manure, lawn sweepings, straw or even loosened earth.

PERENNIALS
Plants which die down each year, but always start growing the following spring (that is to say, if they have not been eaten by slugs, ants, etc.) Perennials are such as daffodils, snowdrops, tulips, lilies of the valley, lupins, montbretia, hollyhock, polyanthus, gladioli, geranium. I am partial to perennials; I like plants that come up with monotonous regularity each year.

ROTATION OF CROPS

The planting of successive crops in a clear and definite order to ensure a suitable supply of food for each. Never mind a suitable supply of food for you.

SHRUBS

Bushy plants which go on year after year after many a long year. They do need pruning, but nevertheless flowering shrubs can be a great joy. In February and March the forsythia will bloom ... or it could be a bit later depending upon the weather. In late May and early June the azaleas and rhododendrons grace the gardens, and from July the hydrangeas will bloom until the frosty season comes along and knocks them for six. And there is the honeysuckle and the lavender and the rowan and the firethorn (pyracantha), not to mention the beautiful blue of the ceanothus (evergreen and deciduous!)

SPIT

This is the depth of the spade. If a gardening book advises you to dig a spit deep it means the depth of the spade. Many a time when I have been digging I have wanted not *a* spit but *to* spit.

2 GARDEN PLANNING

If you would be happy for a week, take a wife;
if you would be happy for a month, kill your pig:
but if you would be happy all your life, plant a garden.
Chinese saying

I cannot emphasise too strongly the need for gardeners to have plans and systems. One must be systematic. It is useless to wander aimlessly around the garden pulling out a weed here and a weed there. That is exactly what I did for many months and was it any wonder that my garden never looked up to scratch? And did I care? Down on your hands and knees if need be, with kneeling mat and trowel and little fork to get at those weeds. Stand up and use the Dutch hoe whenever you can and deal with each section of the garden systematically.

Do this regularly one half day every six weeks and, like me, you could have one small area (two by two) which is weed free and the rest looking as though it gets a bit of aimless weed pulling, which it does. I am the possessor of two lawns; one the size of an afternoon tablecloth and the other the size of a dinner table cloth. How I love hot sizzling summers, but how few we have — hot summers which turn the grass dark brown. Days of rain make me tremble as the wretched green stuff appears to grow before my very eyes.

When planning a garden it is as well to remember that some plants and flowers grow higher than others. For instance, if you plant hollyhocks in front of tulips and forget-me-nots you may as well forget the forget-me-nots and the tulips. Primroses do not really show up behind daffodils. They would not feel too jolly in such a position and neither would you.

On the subject of trees it may be prudent to observe that today's tiny sapling sometimes grows at incredible speed and could tomorrow block out light and air before arranging, in a gale force wind, to fall on your house.

I have had to learn many of these points the hard way. I can advise you to plant tulips in an open but sheltered position. Pull yourself together and make up a depth of two feet with a rich compost of about four parts loam, one part leaf mould and one part of decomposed manure. Thoroughly mix it together — if you have sufficient foresight — some time before it is required.

TULIPS AND ROSES

Prepare the tulip ground in September or early October. Plant bulbs in October or early November six inches apart and three or four inches deep. Place a little river sand around each bulb.

Plants like variety — like a dressing of soot, later on a dash of manure — and later still a drop of guano (which, to the uninitiated, is seabird manure). Roses like a rich deep soil and plenty of air and moisture. Plant roses in the sunniest and most sheltered section of the garden. Horse manure suits the rose and also poultry manure, but do apply sparingly. Very light sand and chalk soils should not attract the would-be rose grower. Do not manure after the second crop of roses begins to show colour. Apply the hoe and a bit of light forking when the flower season is over. Plant roses in November. Taking a cutting and slit one inch upwards at the bottom to insert a grain of wheat. *See also* Page 78 for Cuttings.

CLIMBING PLANTS

Aaah, the scent of honeysuckle — I love the scent it sends forth. Mine flowers from June until October. It has cream, pink-tinged blossoms ... Apparently too heavy pruning could result in the loss of flowers. I did not wish to be deprived of one single blossom so for a long time I did not prune the honeysuckle. Honeysuckle thrives just about anywhere and definitely has a mind of its own. You should give honeysuckle a light feed of rotted compost in March if your soil is poor. I've starved my honeysuckle and it thrives.

If you seek to disguise an ugly wall or plain shed or even the compost heap why not introduce a climbing plant. You cannot make a silk purse out of a sow's ear but you can put a pretty ear muff on it — a dead sow of course.

Ivy does not need any support. It can climb unaided and cling with tenacity. Virginia creeper is much the same. But there are many other climbers which require assistance such as tying or even nailing to fence or shed. If you do have to nail your climber please ensure that as you bend the nail over it doesn't squeeze the plant. Put yourself in the plant's position! If you consider an archway or trellis to act as a support try to imagine how the climber will reduce the width of the area in which you are fixing it. If it's against a fence with yards of lawn or whatever in front of it — well and good. It is something I cannot say too often even if it does make for being a bore — planning is vital. Remember when you're arranging a climber support, wet plants are heavier than dry ones. If it's a clematis you are planting try mixing mortar rubble with the soil. Remember it likes a shady position, so a north or west wall should be ideal. Clematis thrives in chalky loam soil; planting time October to November. Prune drastically each year. Cut back to within about one foot of the ground in February, if your clematis flowers in summer or autumn. Other varieties flower from the old wood so only cut out straggling and weak growth so that it can develop beautifully.

The beautiful wisteria needs plenty of room for root growth. Moist rich soil is best but wisteria will thrive in most soils. However it needs a south or west facing wall or trellis. Prune in February by cutting back to within two or three buds of the actual base of last year's growth. When digging a hole for a climber make it at least three feet by three feet and eighteen inches deep. Fill it with really good soil.

Cover a wall or fence with Virginia Creeper and the beauty of its leaves in autumn will overcome you. So will sweeping up the vast quantities of leaves which it will shed over a period of some weeks.

GARDEN RUBBISH

Waste materials can become a real embarrassment if their accommodation is omitted from the essential planning schedule. Weeds, leaves and lawn mowings should go on to the compost heap. Or you could try chucking them over your neighbour's fence!

Space should be allowed for the never ending collection of rubbish, broken twigs, roots of prolific perennial weeds — such as the dear old convolvulus, dock and dandelion and those diseased leaves: all to be burned (except twigs which will rot into compost eventually) as you accumulate them and they become dry enough. What you need for these waste materials is a utility area, a corner

15

which can be hidden from sight by a trained rambler rose or hedge or I guess a row of runner beans could camouflage it in the veggie garden. Or if you are completely mad hide it behind a row of such shrubs as will have to be kept in order and pruned regularly. But you do need space for a compost heap and a bonfire out of sight of the garden proper.

OTHER CONSIDERATIONS

I know it is said that the scope of a garden is vastly increased if a greenhouse is available. And it increases labour. So maybe you should forget it. Even if no garden can possibly be complete without one. I admit a cold frame or greenhouse can be very useful and the latter is ideal to shelter in from the rain.

Other possibilities: Put plants under big spreading trees or in ground that is ill-prepared and you cannot expect wonderful results. Indeed, you may find your crops leggy, diseased and plagued with caterpillars. If you have branches hanging over from a neighbour's garden and also roots trespassing you should cut them back, provided you can talk amicably to your neighbour. If you are in luck he may come in and cut them back for you. It is as well to avoid the bonfire solution as the smoke may cause annoyance to your neighbours. So if you don't like your neighbours... Plant vegetables and flowers beneath fruit trees and bushes and, as you tangle with the gooseberry bush in trying to reach an undernourished onion, you will wish you had not.

Method is essential in gardening. I cannot repeat this too often. Without method, time and effort can be wasted. Besides method and a utility area a garden shed is essential. You can use it to house tools etc. and sometimes you can use it to hide away. Useful garden tools are spade, fork, hoe, rake, dibber, small fork, small trowel and kneeling mat. Do not forget tools should always be cleaned before being put away and, if you have the strength, do it.

3 M and S
(MANURE and SOIL)
(MUCK and SOD)

The blood of English shall manure the ground,
And future ages groan for this foul act
Shakespeare: Richard II

MANURE

It is not a pretty subject, but of necessity the gardener must get to know his manure. There is organic and inorganic manure, organic being derived from animal or vegetable matter, inorganic being of mineral origin.

Manure when used in moderate quantities can be most beneficial (in strong doses it can injure vegetables). It suits onions, beans, carrots, beetroot, asparagus but remember: *in small quantities.*; little is good. Bulbs will benefit from slight doses of manure. When shovelling in the manure try to mix it as thoroughly as possible with the soil. With light porous soil try manuring in early spring, heavy to heavyish soil in the winter. Someone once told me that peas and beans gather nitrogen from the air and store it; so to apply a manure which is nitrogenous would be a waste of time and money. Well I wasn't too sure what he meant but I've no wish to do either. The lesson is know your manure. And as you survey your estate and take a deep breath you may well ask yourself, "Is it worth it?"

HORSE MANURE
Some horse manure *can* contain shavings and this is not good for the ground on account of it causes fungi. Horse manure which contains straw is splendid stuff for digging into clay or other such

heavy soils. Light soil is rather more responsive to cow or pig manure. Well there are some people who prefer jelly to custard!

FOWL and also PIGEON MANURE

Very strong stuff this and it could do much damage if used too liberally. Store it in the dry in equal parts of dry soil just like a sandwich. Mix it up and powder it down when you require it for growth in the growing season. And you will be glad to know that a trowelful per yard once a fortnight is ample.

An old method with manure is to fill a small sack with manure and suspend it in a barrel of water. This liquid manure will be ready for use in a couple of days.

FARMYARD MANURE

Farmyard manure consists of mixed dung of horses and cattle thrown together and more or less soaked in the liquid drainage of the stable or byre. This is best used in a moderately fermented state.

Going back to horse manure (if you are mad enough to want to) horse dung is very beneficial to cold stiff soils. A bit of warm softening up there! But do not allow it to linger unmoved for too long when fresh, for it will heat up violently and the ammonia will veritably rush off. So try turning it over three or four times. And it definitely should be well moistened, preferably with farmyard drainings.

COW DUNG

This may be less fertilising than horse dung but because it is slower in action it is more durable. If thoroughly decayed it is one of the best manures for mixing in composts for choice plants and flowers.

PIG MANURE

Pig dung is some powerful stuff. It has even more nitrogen than horse dung so for goodness sake mix it with litter and a portion of earth so that it can ferment. It is a well-known fact (although this chicken did not know it until recently) that the drainings from a pig sty provide a valuable manure for vegetable crops.

Incidentally (have you noticed how when anyone has anything important to say they say 'incidentally'?) manure the colour of

weak tea is considered the best.
Tea itself or tea leaves suit hydrangeas.

Farm slurry with worms romping in it produces a very high class manure. The creme de la creme!!

BONES
Bones can be used as manure. They are best on dry soils as food for vegetables, especially turnips and fruit trees.

BURNT CLAY
This is very good for clay soil. Only burn it slightly so that it will crumble readily. Do not let the fire actually burn through; this is what used to be called in my grandfather's day 'smother burning'.

VEGETABLE REFUSE/COMPOST
Decompose the 'veggie' refuse in a heap with quick lime and then layer with earth. With a bit of luck it should turn into compost. Or you can line a wire receptacle with old carpet to keep heat and moisture in; plonk in old veggie refuse, decomposable household refuse (not plastic), crushed eggshells, small twigs, nettles; cover with old carpet or sacking and within a couple of months you should have well rotted compost with only eggshells, twigs and stuff that takes ages to decompose still recognisable.

SOOT
Soot will prevent attacks of insects such as the onion gnat and the turnip fly if you plonk it on the ground *around* onions and turnips or you could try flicking common salt *over* them. Sooty water is beneficial to gardens. A bag of soot put in a tank where water is stored will be a wonderful help. But do not fall into it for it will not do you any good.

SOIL

You must understand your soil. You would wish for a perfect soil. Let me tell you right away, there is no such soil. It is either sandy, stony, dusty or clay.

CLAY

This type of soil needs, nay demands, manure or leaf mould and sand or grit, fire ashes; or charred bits from the bonfire you lit to annoy the neighbours. Dig in deeply (the aforementioned, not yourself). Dig in peat. Scatter lime; fling it around. Clay soil does have its advantages for it retains moisture during periods of drought. It stays really squelchy.

SANDY

You have to dig decaying vegetation or chopped turf or both into this lot. Or, if you live near a brewery, shovel in some spent hops. Or if you live near the sea dig in some seaweed (wet or dry) — it will feel quite at home in the sand besides doing good. When you have dug in these or some of the aforementioned moisture holding items, if you still feel well enough, fork in some crushed chalk, somewhere around one pound to the square yard. (You simply do not get old-fashioned tips in metric.) There are probably advantages to a sandy soil but I cannot think of one except that if your sandy soil garden happens to be on the beach I do know the dreaded slug has no liking for salt.

STONY

This type of soil has good drainage. Dig in some animal manure, or spent hops. If you do not live near a farm or brewery now is your chance to do so. Although you could try digging in the veggie waste or good old seaweed (wet or dry).

DUSTY SOIL

Pack really deeply with moisture providing materials as mentioned previously. Work it in really hard and then even harder (you could get rid of your aggressions this way). Add chopped turf or heavy clay.

DREARY BLACK SOIL

This type of soil is unusually lifeless and makes the gardener feel none too lively either. Lime and more lime is the answer here. And it is best put in during the winter. Again, around one pound to the square yard.

PEAT SOIL

There is nothing for it but to put plenty of lime on this type of soil, and it would be to your advantage, although not to your backache, to mix to a goodly depth a mixture of clay or really heavy loam. Rhododendrons, azaleas, heaths and heathers thrive in peat soil. If you cannot identify the type of soil you are unfortunate enough to have to work, try getting a farm institute or some kindly neighbour to identify it. My soil is a kind of clay. It is not very kind and I now firmly believe that the centre of the earth consists of peat. The many bags I have lugged across and shovelled on my garden over the years...well, it went somewhere.

DIGGING

The art of digging is to do it in a leisurely fashion. Frantic digging is both wasteful and tiring. Be calm. If your wife/husband says you are not progressing swiftly enough hand her/him the spade. If she/he continues to niggle, clout her/him with it.

You dig to break up the soil, bury weeds, cover in manure, let in essential air and open up unused stores of plant food. You, in your small way are making the soil fertile to a greater depth. The best time to dig? Well, it would be inadvisable to try to dig when the ground is covered with snow. When a fall of snow has settled my advice to you is either build a snowman, or sit by the fire.

The best time to dig? When the ground is neither frozen nor so wet that it squelches underfoot. Dig at anytime during the autumn. If you cannot manage it in the autumn, heavy ground should be dug in the early winter and then, with luck, the big unyielding lumps will be crumbled and sweetened by wind and frost.

Lighter soil can be dealt with at any time so there is no excuse there, I am sorry to tell you. For clay soil use a fork.

Stony, gravelly , or sandy soils need the attention of a spade. But whether spade or folk, use a reasonably sized one of medium weight. Not quite so hard on the muscles. The spade blade should be pressed into the ground with the ball of the left foot: unless you are right-footed or left-handed.

Turf contains really valuable plant food. When digging, bury it deeply turfside down. If ,however, turf contains grubs such as wireworms, scatter lime or soot thickly over it before covering it. As soil accumulates on the spade, scrape it off with a piece of wood.

Bastard trenching is not rude like it sounds. Just hard work. It means digging two spits deep and this should be done to one third of the 'veggie' plot each year so that in three years the whole of the patch will have been dug to a depth of approximately three feet. The soil one foot down will be broken up and left where it is and the next trench transferred forward on top of it. This method can considerably improve the prospect of crops but probably shortens the life of the digger. The spade too could give out.

4 LAWNS, HEDGES and WINDOW BOXES

There is no riddle to surpass
The mystery of growing grass
Which bravely thrusts its tender stalk
Thru tiny cracks along the walk,
And thrives in crannies of the wall,
And in the flower beds grows tall
And grows and grows, till summer's gone,
On everything except the lawn.

Curtis Heath

LAWNS

I laughingly refer to 'my lawns' when, in truth, they are simply bits of field, though I do make the odd effort to improve them. To produce a lawn of the finest quality you need really well-drained ground. So that throws me at the first hurdle, having lawns on ground which is boggy in parts and stiff with the dry in others.

On a well drained piece of ground have a good deep dig. Then let the ground settle down and the elements do their part, and good luck to them. When you feel the subsidence is completed try to level the ground and get rid of the roughness and the stones.

Seeding can be done in the spring or autumn. April is considered to be the best month for spring sowing; or late August for autumn sowing. Consult your local grass seed seller for advice on the best type of seed. My grandfather always said one pound of seed mixed with fine soil would be the right amount for each sixteen square yards. Plant and then rake over. Attach black cotton to sticks and criss cross the cotton across the newly sown lawn to protect the seed from the birds.

Old soot, well slaked lime, burnt wood and vegetable ashes are all good for feeding the lawn provided all the aforementioned stuff is well sieved. You can get rid of clover by sprinkling nitrate of soda at the amount of one ounce every square yard. It would save a lot if time if you cemented the ground and painted it green.

September is the time for applying a worm killer to your lawn. Mix one ounce of slaked lime to a gallon of water and use this amount on every square yard. Personally I like the worms to live on and under my lawns because they are aerating the soil, or so I tell myself.

In the autumn you should try leaping over the established lawn with a fork — no, a large garden fork. And make holes in the lawn to aerate it. So I am all for the worms doing it for me.

My lawns harbour clover, dandelion, daisies and buttercups. Rather nice I always think. And I thought it would be rather friendly if I had some nice snowdrops and crocuses to break up the different shades of green in the grass in Spring before the clover, daisies, etc. put in their appearance. I carefully cut the turf around three sides of a square the width of the spade, and rolled it back. Then I planted the snowdrops and crocus bulbs a couple of inches down in a square hole which I had made with my fingers. (I knew I must not plant these bulbs in a pointed hole leaving an air pocket.) Then I carefully rolled back the turf. And then I repeated the action five times. Nothing happened this spring so I'm waiting for next.

There is something very attractive about a turfed path; until you actually have one. For, sad to relate, a turfed path needs frequent mowing and weeding. As if you don't get enough of that from the lawn itself. Please take note, if you must cut flower beds in the lawn and if their shapes are fanciful, or even just oval, their edges will require frequent trimming. If you must cut a flower bed in the lawn I would suggest you do so in a discreet place: like behind a giant variety garden gnome, lying prone.

Bone meal will get rid of moss — sprinkle it over the lawn, *after* you have dragged the moss out with a rake. Always wear gloves when handling bonemeal. Dumps and bumps in the lawn can only be remedied by lifting the turf and adding or removing soil as required and then replacing the turf. It is all too much for me so I stick with the dumps and the bumps now; although on one occasion I did decide I would do something about the huge bumps that appeared on my lawn. Even to my untrained eye and ignorant eyes, those lumps were quite obviously mole hills. I looked at them with interest, trepidation and wonder. Mole hills bumping across my front lawn. But no! Said my knowledgable neighbour, they were 'anthills'. Well, I knew how to kill ants — boiling water. I boiled up kettle after kettle and raced around the lawn pouring wildly. On my fourth trip to refill the kettle and boil up, my neighbour said, quite gently, "You will kill the grass".

"Never mind," I replied blithely, "there is very little grass there anyway."

But, from the numerous brown patches that appeared later, my lawn I must have had rather more grass than I realized. I would have been wiser if I had plonked inverted pots (covering the hole in the pot) over the nest and poured cold water around the rims each day. A few days later, a part of the nest would have transferred to the pot. Then I could have gingerly slipped a square of cardboard or plastic under the pot and dropped it into salted water.

An easy plan for replacing bare patches on the lawn is as follows: when you are weeding those wretched beds and borders you will espy that there are small gentle tufts of grass growing where they should not grow; remove them gently. Make the soil in the bare patches a bit loose, and put the dear little tufts over the bare patch about two inches apart. They will soon make themselves at home there. Sometimes the edges of the lawn become trodden, and look none too pretty, so if you are feeling energetic, remove the broken edge in a foot wide strip, turn it right around, and then put it back, putting the cut edge down first, with the broken edge going inside. Now roll it. Then go and lie down.

HEDGES

A hedge needs, as with everything in the gardening world, careful planning. Do you seek a laurel hedge which is evergreen? If, when you are cutting it, you cut a leaf in half, that half left will discolour. However, it does make a nice firm thick hedge. Privet is a favourite. We once had a long golden privet hedge. It was beautiful. You can achieve a tall hedge with cypress or a low hedge with lavender. Lavender has a nostalgic perfume of course. And attracts bees keenly.

Like a house, a hedge need a good foundation. Mark out your planting site, and then dig it at least two feet wide and eighteen inches deep. Dig in decayed compost stuff throughout that depth. Leave the soil to settle down for weeks. Give it a rest, and yourself.

Make planting holes about nine inches apart. After planting cut back to within about nine inches of the ground. This will encourage the plants to bush out. Cut back again down to nine inches when they have reached twelve inches. Constant watering in spring and early summer will I fear be absolutely necessary. Keep the area around the roots free from weeds. Clip the hedge occasionally to encourage bushiness. And when it reaches the desired height I'm afraid you will have to cut it frequently and harshly.

You will also have to pick up your clippings. However, if you spread sacking or similar along the side of the hedge before you proceed to cut this will ease the burden.

If you achieve a gap in your hedge, do not despair. This has happened several times in my lavender hedge. Dig out the old roots and the tired soil as well. Then plant a young plant in the offending gap. It will soon bridge that gap.

WINDOW BOXES

Do not have a window box so that it obscures the light completely, or indeed so that it blocks out any light unless you have it in abundance. Think carefully whether or not the outside world immediately below your window box could be disadvantaged when you attend to the needs of the pretty little garden, for example, when watering. Does your window sill slope? Is your window box likely to slip overboard. Make sure it is secure, or you and others could be very unhappy.

The wood for your window box should be between three quarters and one inch thick. Depth can be between seven and nine inches and the length can be the length of the sill. For drainage purposes you will need half inch holes in the bottom at spaces of roughly nine inches. The length of the box should be such that it fits easily between the sides of the opening. Place wedges underneath the box to make it level on the tray to catch surplace water.

Fix hooks or similar on the sides so that the box can be secured to the walls or woodwork; the bottom of the box should not touch the sill. Paint it any colour that grabs you. Burn paper to char the inside (before you install it) as this will prevent rot. But do not set fire to it. Place a two inch layer of small stones at the bottom. Cover these with reversed turf or leaf mould or even leaves. About an inch in depth. Fill with good soil to within an inch of the top.

Plant snowdrops, crocuses, grape hyacinth. Depending on the time of year, begonias can make a lovely show, as can pansies, stocks, lobelia, or geranium. Daffodils too can make a good show but may block your window. Fuchsias pushing through a carpet of forget-me-nots look beautiful. Polyanthus or primroses are pretty good too. The choice is yours. But I do hope your window opens inwards. For you may need to water the window box every day.

Heathers can also provide a gladdening sight. Indeed, your window box can be a miniature garden in every way. And don't think the slugs won't think so too.

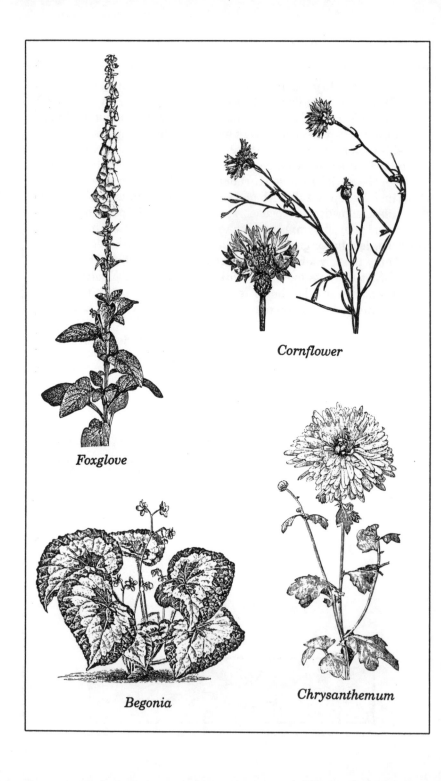

Foxglove

Cornflower

Begonia

Chrysanthemum

5 THE FLOWER GARDEN

The kiss of the sun for pardon,
The song of the birds for mirth,
One is nearer Gods heart in a garden,
Than anywhere else on earth.

Dorothy Gurney, 1858 - 1932

ANEMONE
Perennial. Flowers in spring. Comes in a variety of colours. Will grow up to twelve inches. Plant six inches deep and three inches apart in September or October. Will grow well in moderate shade. Good for floral arrangement. A corm called St Brigid is the most popular.

AQUILEGIA (Granny Bonnets)
Hardy perennial. Flowers from May to August. Variety of colours. Height one to three feet. Sow seeds in June or propagate; plant by division of clumps in October or March. Does really well in semi-shade. Provides many graceful blooms for cutting.

ASTER
Half hardy annual. Flowering season from August to October. Single and double varieties. Comes in a variety of colours. Can grow from six inches up to eighteen inches. Grown from seed. Plant in boxes in frame or greenhouse in March. Plant outdoors in April or sow seeds outdoors in April. Likes rich soil with well rotted manure.

AUBRETIA
Hardy perennial evergreen. Blooms through spring into early summer. Available in rose, mauve, lavender, violet, and purple. Seldom exceeds four inches in height. Provides carpeting, edging

or planting in the rockery. Sow seed in May to June in the open or in a box in frame for flowering the following year. Cut back dramatically if required, after flowering. Soft root tips of growth taken in June root freely in a shady frame.

BEGONIAS

Half hardy perennial (tuberous rooted or fibrous rooted). Summer flowering through to frost in autumn. Wide variety of colours. Height about eighteen inches, but some varieties grow to twelve inches. Suitable for summer bedding and growing in pots. Plant late — May to June — twelve inches apart in rich soil. Full sunshine not essential. The twelve inch tall variety is suitable for filling or edging summer beds or for window boxes or flower pots. They should not lack water. Both varieties can be grown from seed or from cuttings taken in the spring. Stored tubers (see page 90) should be potted up in March/April, kept moist and in a warm atmosphere. Harden off for planting outdoors in May/June.

CARNATION

Hardy perennial. Flowers in summer and provides a quantity of long-stemmed blooms for cutting. Considerable range of colours. Height about two feet. Perfumed. Plant in September to October or early spring. Soil should be well dug and drained with lime added if necessary. Plant about eighteen inches apart in sunny position. Make soil quite firm around these plants. May remain undisturbed for three to four years. Stakes may be necessary because these plants can become top heavy. Replace by layering when necessary. To increase size of bloom 'disbud', that is to say, each flowering stem should be allowed to carry only one flower).

CHERRY PIE (Heliotrope)

Half hardy perennial. Flowers in summer. Comes in lilac and purple. Has a scent like stewed cherries. Height up to two feet. May need staking. It is adapted to pot culture. Requires sunny position and good soil. Sow seed in heated greenhouse in March to April for planting out in May. Must be over-wintered in a frost-free greenhouse, kept fairly dry and, in February, the withered tips and side shoots should be cut back.

CHRYSANTHEMUM

There are several varieties — annuals, half hardy perennials and hardy perennials. So take you pick! They grow outdoors from summer through to Christmas but the season can be extended under greenhouse conditions. They come in all the lovely colours and can be single or double, incurved or shaggy or 'spider' blooms. Can grow from one foot to four feet. They do not like poor soil. Plant eighteen inches apart and stake taller plants. Propagate by sowing or taking cuttings.

CORNFLOWER

Annual or perennial flowers and neither variety needs much in the way of cultivation! Summer flowering annuals can be blue, pink, purple or white. Hardy perennials can be blue, white or yellow depending on the variety. Grow up to three feet. Sow seed in March outdoors. When they put in an appearance thin out to six inches apart. Too rich soil can cause perennials to have good growth but poor flowers. Propagate perennials by dividing the clumps.

CROCUS

Hardy bulbous plant. Flowers in the early spring. Wide variety of colours including purple, white and yellow. Grows up to six inches. Ideal for border, rockery or even in the lawn. Plant bulbs three inches deep and three inches apart between October and December. The bulbs can be left in the ground for four to five years, then lifted for division of bulbs in June or July. Store in mice- proof conditions until planting time. New plants can be raised from seed but will take three or four years before flowering.

CYCLAMEN

Hardy outdoor *or* popular greenhouse variety. Hardy outdoor will flower in spring and autumn. Indoor variety flowers from November to late April. Wide variety of colours. Hardy outdoor will grow to four inches high. Sow seeds in the spring or plant corms for both varieties in August or September. Protect from hot sun and wind. Sow close to shrubs or similar.
Indoor variety has dormant period from April to August when plants should be kept fairly dry.

DAFFODIL

Hardy perennial. Spring flowering. Most popular colours are yellow or white. They grow to approximately one foot high. Plant bulbs in October four inches below the soil, spaced four to six inches apart. After flowering wait until foliage is quite withered and will come away with a slight tug. Then tug out those withered leaves. If you need space for summer occupants replant in odd spot until foliage has completely died. Then lift and store until October planting time. Clumps can be left for three to four years, but then lift and divide bulbs and re-plant.

DAHLIA

Perennial but not hardy. Flowers from August until the first frost. Wide variety of colours. They vary in height from one foot to five feet depending on variety. Plant tubers or cuttings when there is no fear of frost. Plant from three to four feet apart or eighteen inches for the smaller variety. Rich soil dug deep is required. Propagation is by taking cuttings or division of tubers. They should be lifted late autumn unless weather really mild, and stored in frost free situation. Dahlias originated in Mexico.

EVENING PRIMROSE

Hardy biennial and perennial varieties. Summer flowering. Expect an abundance of blooms in lovely shades of yellow. Can range from four inches to four feet in height. Sow seeds outdoors in June for planting out in autumn or spring. Propagation by self-seeding and the perennials are best cared for by cutting back in the autumn and lifting and dividing clumps after three years.

FORGET-ME-NOT

Hardy biennial. Spring flowering. Common varietries are blue or pink. Normally grow to six inches high. Sow seed in June, outdoors, transplant seedlings in autumn to their flowering position for the following spring. Self-seeding. Normally will accept most soils but in dry weather they expect plenty of water.

FOXGLOVE

Hardy biennial. Spring flowering. Blooms usually in white or purple. Can grow from four to six feet high. Sow seed in June or July outdoors for flowering position for the following spring.

Flourish in a damp, slightly shady position as well as in full sun, and if left to its own devices will re-seed itself.

FREESIA

Half hardy perennial. Distinctive perfume. Summer flowering or winter and spring if indoors. Variety of colours. Height about twelve inches. Plant corms in pots in good soil one inch deep and two inches apart in August onwards in heated greenhouse for flowering in winter and spring. Staking will be necessary. Seed may be sown in heated greenhouse from January to March for flowering the following summer. Plant outside only when there is no fear of frosts. Must over-winter in a green house or indoors.

FUCHSIA

Hardy and half hardy perennials. Summer flowering until the first frost. Tremendous variety of colours and shapes — mauve, pink, reds, white, orange, and tans. From one foot to six feet in height *so check on variety*. It is important to seek a sunny position in good soil. Plant end of May or early June at least twelve inches apart. Soil must be kept reasonably moist at all times. Propagate by seeds sown in greenhouse or by cuttings. Lift non-hardy plants in September or October and keep in frost free area with plenty of light. Hardy plants can stay outdoors and some species make good hedges; it is some of the hardy variety which grow to six feet.

GERANIUM

Hardy and half hardy perennial. Flowering time is from May to July. Colours range from white to pale pink to deep purple and include variegated varieties. Can grow from four inches to two feet depending on variety. Shorter variety suit rockery in full sun. Taller variety suit mixed border. Half hardy plants will need over-wintering indoors in frost free conditions (although they can survive a mild winter). Trailing variety is suitable for hanging baskets. Seeds can be sown in heated conditions in January.

Plant outside in May or early June at least nine inches apart in not too rich soil conditions or the leaves will submerge the flower. If drying winds or strong sun occur during the first week after planting, lightly shield with newspaper of similar. Lift in October and store in full light but frost-free conditions. These plants lifted from the garden will need roots and top growth cut back. Pot in light soil. Those plants kept in pots or hanging baskets will also need top growth trimming. Keep soil just moist enough to prevent roots shrivelling. Remove dying leaves. Be sure the foliage is kept free of moisture.

Take cuttings (short hard feeling side shoots tinged with red: an indication of ripeness) from best of the parent plants in August, early September, or early spring. You can then can dispose of parent plants if you so desire. Propagation can also be by division of roots in autumn or spring, and by seeds sown outdoors in early summer.

GLADIOLA

Hardy bulbous perennial. Flowering season from June to September. Very wide variety of colours. Super for flower arranging. Height up to three feet or more. Seed can be sown in February in heated conditions but will take three years before flowering!!! The most popular method is to plant corms in March six inches apart and three inches below the surface. Use a trowel rather than a dibber so that they are sitting on a flat base and not a point. You can grow them in a patch of their own for cutting or they look lovely in clumps in a mixed border. The ground should be well dug and enriched with stable manure or well rotted compost. When corms are lifted at the end of the season, separate baby corms (known as offsets) and store for planting in March. I leave mine in the ground.

GYPSOPHILA

Hardy annual and perennial varieties. Summer flowering. Colours include white and pink. Pretty but very tiny flowers. Height up to four feet. Sow annual type seeds in March or April where you desire them to flower. Seedlings when they appear should be thinned out to four to six inches apart. Sow perennial type seeds in June in open or in cold frame. Set the young plants out in the autumn in the place you want them to flower in the following year. Or ,if you are starting out with perennial plants put them in during the autumn. Propagation can be by cuttings in spring. Light soil and dryish position is appreciated.

Gypsophila in a flower arrangement compliments a variety of other flowers most expecially sweet peas and it can be dried for winter use.

HOLLYHOCK

Hardy perennial. Summer flowering for many weeks. Wide variety of colours in single and double types. Can grow to a height of ten feet so do plant at the back of your border. Needs plenty of head room and sunshine. Good soil deeply dug is required. Planting time is April; keep the plants at least eighteen inches apart. Summer treatment: Staking is a prime factor and do it before there can be any wide damage. Watch out for the rust spots and treat (*see* pest section). In autumn cut plant right down and leave only the bottom growths. Will self seed if dead flowers are left on the plant. Otherwise remove pods and sow seeds in June.

HONESTY

Hardy biennial. Purple or white flowers in early summer. But mainly grown for their winter floral arrangements as their silvery white seedpods are so decorative. Height approximately two feet. Propagation: self-seeding, but seeds can be sown in June in the open or in a box in a frame. Seedlings should be set out in a spare patch until they can be planted in the border in early autumn for flowering the following summer.

IRIS

Hardy perennial. Depending on variety flowers from April to early summer. Variety of colours including blue, yellow and a beautiful brown. Height up to two feet. Needs a well drained position in full sun if possible. They do like to have lime in the soil and if the soil is of a heavy variety you should lighten it. Plant the root stocks (rhizomes) in July to August, or September to October at the latest. However, failing this, you can plant them in early March. The rhizomes should be left half exposed. Planting should be in clumps and should not be lifted for three to four years (yippee) but lift and divide after flowering to increase stock, if you wish.

Winter Treatment: stiff blades of foliage wither in autumn and winter so cut these back without damage to the new young growth which hopefully is shooting. *If* the withered blades are allowed to droop to soil level they provide homes for and hidey holes for slugs and snails during the winter.

NB: Other rhyzome varieties (such as the beardless and the Japanese) require damp conditions. And there are bulbous irises,

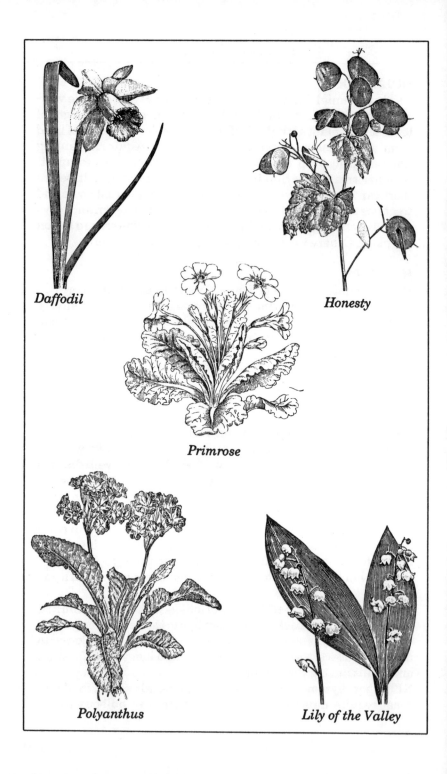

Daffodil

Honesty

Primrose

Polyanthus

Lily of the Valley

which can be planted in August to October and can grow to a few inches or to two feet high depending on the type. The bulbous varieties can also be left in for three years, when the offsets can be lifted in the same way as the gladioli offsets.

LILY
Hardy perennial bulbous. Summer flowering. Various colours, but three of the most well known are the Arum and the Madonna which are white and the Tiger which is a sort of apricot/ orange colour. Some varieties grow to two feet tall but there are others that grow up to six feet. So it is important to check variety. Distinctive heady perfume. Plant in October, preferably in clumps six inches apart and six inches deep. Bulbs should be left in the ground undisturbed for as many years as possible. Natural increase could in time make the clumps overcrowded. When this happens the bulbs should be lifted when the tops have withered in the autumn and re-planted in soil which has been enriched with manure or leaf mould. Be generous with watering in dry weather and feed sparingly with liquid manure throughout the growing season.

Lilies are best planted in light soil but will thrive in heavy soil provided that at the bottom of each planting hole a handful of sharp grit or sand has been placed for the bulb to rest on. In heavy soil conditions it is also best to surround the whole of the bulb with the aforementioned type of material. Propagation: offsets of baby bulbs which you remove from old bulbs when these are lifted in autumn. Re-plant one inch deep and two inches apart in light soil outdoors in box in a frame for planting out the following autumn. Seed is available but will take three or more years to flower.

LILY OF THE VALLEY
Hardy perennial. Beautiful fragrance. Spring flowering. Colour white; dark green leaf. Height six to nine inches. Popular cut flower and popular in the herbaceous border. Will grow in shady patch but not if gloomy and overhung by bushes. Will also grow in a semi shady spot for early flowering. May be difficult to establish but once settled they grow profusely. Plant crowns during September and October just below the surface in soil well prepared by using leaf mould or old manure. Water generously

during dry periods and give fortnightly doses of liquid manure or fertiliser during the summer.

Winter treatment: an inch of leaf mould or rotted manure should be beneficial. After several years they may get overcrowded, so may need digging up, dividing and replanting. Propagation: the most popular way is by dividing clumps, planting biggest crowns together and nurturing smaller crowns in a separate patch.

LUPIN

Hardy annual, hardy perennial and hardy tree lupin. Flower in summer. Variety of colours. The annual usually grow to two feet and perennials to two to three feet but tree lupins., which look rather like a bush, can grow to five feet.

Annuals: sow seed thinly in required situation in March to April to flower that summer. Thin out seedlings to eighteen inches apart.

Perennial: plant in spring or autumn in groups of three or four separated by eighteeen inches. Stake before wind can wreak havoc. Look out for slugs and snails for they like to clamber up the stalks and nibble away. Cut down stems in October. Leave in ground for four or five years, then lift: and rooted side shoots should be planted in spring. But seed may also be sown in open frame in June for plants the following year.

Tree Lupin: sow seed in June outdoors or in a frame for flowering the following year. Should the frost cut back growth do not worry for new growth should arrive at the base in the spring. Should top growth survive the winter trim into shape in the spring.

MARIGOLD

Hardy annual. Flowers from June to late autumn. Several varieties including French, African and Old English. There are doubles and singles and mainly vary from clear lemon to orange but can be obtained in various other colour combinations. Can grow from six inches to three feet depending on variety. Sow seed outdoors from April to May in flowering position. And they will flower within weeks! Drastic thinning out of seedling to at least a foot apart is necessary. With the French and African variety earlier flowering and stronger plants are assured by planting the seed in a warm greenhouse in March. They *will* survive a drought, though they do appreciate water. Dead heading will improve the length of flowering time for all three varieties. Best to cut the dead heads off rather than break them.

MONTBRETIA

Hardy perennial bulbous. Flowers August to September. Variety of colours including orange, yellow and scarlet. Height up to three feet. Look attractive massed in a mixed border and are also used in cut flower arrangements. Should be planted two inches apart and three inches deep in March. Allegedly should be lifted and re-planted each year *or,* if left in ground, put on old manure in March. Mine seem to thrive on neglect. Propagation: produce offsets which can be separated and re-planted. Will grow in most types of soil.

NARCISSUS

Hardy perennial bulbous. Ideal for spring flowering or even extra early flowering indoors in pots. Wide selection of colours. Height up to two feet. Some varieties are highly perfumed. *See* DAFFO-DIL for culture.

NASTURTIUM

Hardy annual (can be self-seeding). Flowers throughout summer and autumn. Mainly yellowy colour. Can be tiny or the climbing variety can grow up to ten feet. Some varieties are delicately perfumed. Will grow reasonably well in poor soil. Seed may be sown outdoors from April to May in position for flowering. The seeds are quite big and should be sown singly one inch deep and not less than nine inches apart. They need lots of water in dry weather and are prevalent to black fly or greenfly. To prevent self-seeding, the seed pods should be picked off daily. If the pods are not picked off there will be loss of flowers. You can make a delicious pickle with nasturtium seeds, as described in my book, *Gran's Old-Fashioned Remedies, Wrinkles and Recipes.*

PANSY

Hardy annual (can be self-seeding). Summer and winter flow-ering. Wide variety of colours. Height up to six inches. Prefers position in life which is shady on a hot day. Requires ample water in dry spells. Appreciates liquid manure and really enjoys a rich soil. If you pick off the blooms as they fade this will prevent self-seeding. Watch out for cuckoo spit or greenfly. Sow seed in June. Put out plants in October or March.

PETUNIA

Hardy annual. Summer flowering. Wide variety of colours with single or double blooms. Height up to twelve inches. In pots up to eighteen inches. Propagation. Seed may be sown in April in sunny frame or greenhouse *or* earlier in heated greenhouse. Plant out in June in rich soil in sunny position approximately nine inches apart. It is possible to take cuttings from plants which have been overwintered in a heated greenhouse.

PHYSALIS (or CHINESE LANTERN / GOOSEBERRY)

Hardy perennial. Summer/Autumn flowering. Has large lantern-shaped flowers that turn red to orange in the autumn. Grows to two feet. Sow seed in April in ordinary garden soil that is well drained. Transplant seedlings to a nursery bed putting them six inches apart when large enough to handle. Later plant eighteen inches to two feet apart in flowering position in summer. Often dried and used for flower arrangements. Cut fruiting stems when lanterns (or gooseberries) begin to show colour. Hang them upside down in bunches in a light airy shed to dry. When stems and fruits are dry remove withered leaves.

PINKS

Hardy perennial. Summer flowering. Wide range of colours in spite of name. Grows to about twelve inches high. Gorgeous scent. Prolific flowering. Put out plants in autumn or spring in good soil with plenty of lime. In fact, if not too much lime in soil add lime at time of planting. Plant nine inches apart. Summer treatment: remove faded flowers promptly, keep roots moist at all times. Weak liquid manure or fertiliser given from May onwards will be appreciated. Replace by layering or pipings when necessary. Seed can be sown for flowering the following year. Rockery pinks which only grow to two or three inches also look good in the front of a border. And some flower as early as April until May.

POLYANTHUS

Hardy perennial. Spring flowering. Very wide choice of colours. Height six to twelve inches. Sow seed outdoors in June. When big enough to handle move seedlings to good soil and place six inches apart ready for planting out in the autumn. In the autumn plant nine inches apart for flowering the following spring. Propagation. After flowering the plants should be lifted, divided and replanted in a reserve spot for planting in flowering position the following autumn. They enjoy being moved twice a year (bit of the itinerant about these). This is a very popular bedding and border plant.

POPPY

Hardy annual and hardy perennial. Flowers during summer. Many shades of pink and red. Can grow up to and between three and four feet depending on variety.
Annual: single and double. Sow seeds in successive batches from March to May and you should get flowers all summer. Sow thinly and shallowly in groups and then thin out to nine inches apart. Perennial: plant roots in October or March in good soil two feet apart, widely and to the back of the mixed border. Or sow seed any time from May to August outdoors to secure plants for placing in flowering position in Autumn or Spring. In late autumn cut back old stems of perennials to the base growth.

PRIMROSE, Common

Hardy perennial. Colour: lovely shades of lemon. *See* POLYAN-THUS for culture.

PYRETHRUM

Hardy perennial. Flowers spring and early summer. Single and double flowers in a variety of lovely colours. Will grow to two feet or more. Plant roots in spring or in August. If you choose August they will flower the following year. Rich soil is desirable. Plant in clumps spaced approximately sixteen inches apart. Staking may be necessary at full growth. Cut back the old growth in the autumn. Lift and divide clumps every third year. Propagation: root division in spring or August is a sure way of increasing your stock. Make the division from the top downwards with a very sharp knife. Or you can sow seed in June to flower the following year. There is also a foliage or ornamental leaf variety which is popularly called Golden Feather. A hardy perennial, it grows to about six inches. Similar propagation treatment as flowering pyrethrum.

ROSE

Hardy perennial. Flowers June to December. Vast variety of colours. They can grow from a few inches to ten feet. There is a large range and many types of rose. For example climbing, rambler, bush and floribunda to mention but a few. Each is beautiful in its own way and some are perfumed. Some varieties leave large handsome hips in the autumn.

Roses like rich soil and plenty of air. Preferably plant in the autumn but you can plant from October to March. Dig ground two feet deep and enrich soil with old (not new) manure or rotted material from the compost heap. The hole should be wide enough and large enough to accept the roots as wide as possible. A newly planted bush rose should be pruned so that it is left with not more than three or four dormant leaf buds. Thorough soaking is necessary in dry weather.

Feed by spreading a layer of rotted farmyard or stable manure over the root area in early spring. Drastic pruning is essential in October to prevent winter gale damage and final pruning should be carried out in March. Summer pruning can be effected by cutting long stems on flowers above bud growth.

My Great-Grandmother's country garden had the most lovely old-fashioned scented roses which no longer exist. But Zephyrine Drouhin a beautiful deep pink climber which was imported into England in mid-nineteenth century still flourishes in my garden. It has the most lovely perfume. Other beautifully scented roses which I can recommend are Beautiful Britain (a lovely pinky red), Rosy Cheeks (pink and white), Queen Elizabeth (deep pink), Freedom (yellow), Albas and Bourbon which are varieties of old roses (white to pink), Peace (lemon with pink), China Town (deep yellow) and Congratulations (rose pink).

Do you know the difference between a rambler and a climber? A rambler has one grand fling each year when it throws forth a profusion of blooms but the climber flowers perpetually throughout the summer and autumn. The rambler was not introduced into the west until the late nineteenth century.

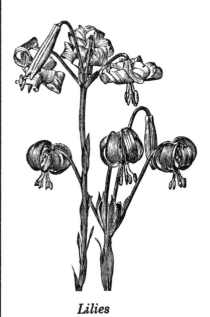

Lilies

Cyclamen

Roses

Gladiolus

SNOWDROP

Hardy perennial bulbous. Flowering season from January to March. Colour White. Grows six to nine inches. Plant from September to December two inches deep and one inch apart; in sunlight or slight shade. Propagation: increase by small bulbs produced as offsets by the older larger ones. Bulbs should however be left undisturbed until they show general signs of debility, eg. lack of flowers. Directly after flowering lift and separate. You can sow seeds outdoors in frame in June. But this way you will have to wait three years for them to flower.

Your man may say, 'I would go through fire and water for you but the roads are icy so I can't come out tonight.' Snowdrops will push their little heads up through the ground in January come ice or snow. They are so dependable.

SOLOMON'S SEAL

Hardy perennial. Flowers from May onwards. Colour white like the white snowdrops. Height two feet. This plant does not mind partial shade. Increases by division of roots which may be done in October or March.

STATICE

Hardy annual or hardy perennial. Flowering season summer to autumn.

Annual: variety of colours including white, rose or blue. Height twelve to eighteen inches. Sow seed in March or April in flowering position and thin out to nine inches apart as and when required. Perennial: variety of colours including white and blue. Height eighteen inches to two feet although the dwarf variety, which lends itself to the rockery, only grows to eight inches high. Plant in March; propagate by root division in March or seed sown in June. However, the seed will only provide plants for flowering the following year. Statice is attractive in the garden and useful for dried flower decoration.

STOCK

Half hardy annual or half hardy biennial. Summer flowering. Variety of colours; gorgeous scent. Grows ten to eighteen inches high.

Annual: sown in March will flower in early June and July.

Biennial: sow seed in March for flowering the following year. To keep the plant flowering remove seed pods as they appear. Needs good soil. Water well in dry periods. Plenty of light and air essential. Enjoys liquid manure during the flowering period.

SUNFLOWER
Hardy annual and hardy perennial. Summer flowering. Can be red, yellow and also bronze. Height twelve inches to ten feet or more But the annual does not grow beyond four feet. Ordinary good soil is required. Plenty of water in dry times.
Annual: sow seed in April to May where the plants are to flower. Perennial: sow plants in October giving space to breathe as they grow up. New thick roots will soon cover a wide area and produce plants further along. Propagation is by division of roots or sowing seed in the spring. Also, early in the winter, cut down old stems and dig up those plants that have wandered too far.

SWEET PEA
Annual. Most lovely fragrance. Flowers early through to late summer. Variety of colours. Grow to height of eight to ten feet. My grandfather who was a keen rugby fan always grew his sweet peas up string netting fixed between two posts rather like goal posts. Good soil enriched with rotted manure or old material from the compost heap is extremely beneficial. Sow seeds in the autumn or early spring in seed boxes in frame as they need protection from the frost. Plant out in March in suitable soil conditions. Take care not to disturb the soil around the roots. Weeding and watering is essential during the summer. And, to encourage flowering, remove seed pods as they appear. Picking the flowers prolongs the flowering season. Staking by cane or twiggy sticks will be required unless you have goal posts like my grandfather did.

SWEET WILLIAM
Hardy biennial. Early summer flowering. Various colours and mixtures of colours. Height eighteen inches. Sow seed outdoors May to July for flowering the following year. When the seedlings are large enough to handle, plant them six inches apart in a nursery bed. Move them in autumn to flowering bed (for the following year) twelve inches apart and in good soil. This is a nice flower for admiring in the garden or in a vase.

TULIP

Hardy perennial bulbous. Spring to summer flowering depending on variety. Variety of colours. Height from a few inches (dwarf variety) to twenty four inches. Plant October to December but preferably October. Can lift after flowering if desired and re-plant on spare patch and water if necessary to allow them to continue their growing cycle. When the tops begin to yellow they can be lifted and stored somewhere safe from mice. They can be left in the ground in winter if the soil is well drained, for a season or two but it is best to lift them each year, dry and store and then replant. Propagation is by tulip offsets which can be separated from the main bulb and planted in good soil. But they will not flower for three to four years.

VIOLET

Hardy perennial. Spring flowering. Variety of colours including blue, purple and white. Single and double blooms. Delicious scent. Grow to a few inches high. Plant during early May in good soil in north-facing position at least nine inches apart for flowering the following spring. Rich soil is necessary. And violets, whether flowering or lying dormant, like cool moist conditions. They send out runners which should be cut off except those required for propagation. Increase of stock can also be made by division of roots immediately after flowering. Seed can be sown in June.

WALLFLOWER

Hardy annual and hardy biennial. Flowers all summer. Extensive range of colours. Single and double blooms and highly perfumed. Height twelve to eighteen inches. But the very popular Siberian wallflower variety only grows from nine to twelve inches, is orange coloured and was always a favourite in a bed interspersed with forget-me-nots and tulips. Seed is sown in June and planted out in a nursery bed, six inches apart in a well drained patch. Strong bushy plants should be planted out in the autumn in their final position in rich soil well drained ground; a sprinkling of lime would be beneficial. Bed the plants in firmly and if frost lifts them tread them back in even more firmly.

WINTER HELIOTROPE

Hardy perennial. Flowers January to March. Pale lilac flowers; plant grows to twelve inches. Beautiful fragrance. To encourage early winter flowering the rhizomes should be planted in autumn just an inch below the surface in a sunny position. Propagation by root division preferably in the autumn.

ZINNIA

Half hardy annual. Summer flowering. Colours include white, yellow and scarlet. Single and double varieties; large flowers. Plant can grow up to two and a half feet tall. Plant out in late May eighteen inches apart in rich soil which has been well manured and deeply dug. Plenty of water in dry weather and staking is essential because of the fragility of the stems. Propagation: sow seeds in frame or greenhouse in April or in the open in early May. Long stem zinnias are lovely in a vase but super in the garden as well.

ERICAS (HEATHERS)

Heathers like peaty soil and plenty of air and light which is why they grow so well on the moors. However, you can grow them in your garden if you so wish and by careful selection using knowledge of their flowering habits you can have some bloom all the year around. Some are best loved for their foliage colouring. Generally speaking they like lime free soil.

6   DISEASES AND REMEDIES

One thing about gardening...you always get a result.
It can be a good or a bad result but it's a result

V A Lethbridge

REMEDIES AGAINST ENEMIES OF FLOWERING PLANTS

It's no good shutting your eyes to those pests and diseases that are setting about your flower display and your crops. They won't go away on their own but will only get worse and ruin the picture and cause a reduction in your yields. As the saying goes 'prevention is better than cure' so as my old gran used to say, "you had better put your heart in the middle of your body and strike the first blow." Or failing that, the advice is: attack early.

At the first sign of activity by biting, creeping, crawling, flying or sucking nasties; 'them what are against your crops and flowers' or, if you observe the onslaught by disease apply the appropriate remedy promptly and thoroughly. Immediate burning of all diseased portions of plants and affected roots and all picked off foliage covered with green or black fly is essential. If you bung it in the refuse tip instead of burning it the heat generated will become a breeding ground for further trouble. No woody rubbish should ever be left lying around. Bits of old stake and rotting wood do not actually breed woodlice and snails but they provide a superb nursery for these pests. A plot that is weedy is an encouragement to all forms of animate and inanimate trouble. And don't I know it.

Alas, there is no cure-all remedy, but listed below are a few help mates. Bordeaux solution, Derris liquid, Flowers of sulphur, Nicotine solution, Pyrethrum solution, Tar oil, Paraffin emulsion, Derris liquid should kill many marauding unfriendly insects.

DERRIS LIQUID
If you decide to spray with derris, mix one ounce of derris power, a quarter of a pound of soft soap with three gallons of water. Dissolve soft soap in a little hot water then mix all the ingredients together.

NICOTINE SOLUTION
Kills green and black fly and certain other small animate pests). Half fluid ounce of nicotine, half a pound of soft soap, five gallons of water (mix soft soap with a little hot water first, to dissolve it). NB: Nicotine is a poison but when diluted as above, its poisonous qualities are not long lasting *but* when spraying flowers make sure it does not get onto other edible crops such as lettuce or cabbage.

PARAFFIN EMULSION
Handful of soft soap stirred in sufficient hot water to dissolve it. Add cool water to make up to amount of two gallons and then add wine glass full of paraffin. Agitate well and spray with syringe.

As a good all round insecticide to deter all pests, my grandfather always used a solution of quassia and soft soap. He used it as hot as his hand could bear.

DISEASES WHICH ARE PECULIAR TO CERTAIN FLOWERS

ASTERS
Black leg disease; remove plant and burn. Lime the ground. Wrinkling of young leaves and growing plants caused by green fly; syringe forcibly with pyrethrum solution.

BEGONIA (INDOOR)
Darkish streaks on underside of leaf caused by whitish green thrip; also growing points attacked by mites which make the

leaves rusty: isolate infected plants and fumigate greenhouse. Greenfly on leaves: spray with pyrethrum solution.

CARNATIONS
Badly spotted and blotched leaves: cut off affected leaves and burn them. Dust the plant with flowers of sulphur. Mildew on leaves: check the disease by dusting with sulphur. Swollen stems caused by eel worm: plants may collapse. Remove plants complete with roots and earth and burn. Fumigate surrounding soil.

CHRYSANTHEMUMS (*Also* CINERARIA)
Leaves tunnelled by grubs: remedy as for beet (*see* page 73). Growing points attacked by greenfly and blackfly: spray or dust with pyrethrum solution. Small reddish circles of rust: pick off and burn leaves and dust with sulphur.

DAHLIA
Buds and blooms eaten by earwigs: *see* page 71.

DELPHINIUM AND LUPIN
Buds and blooms eaten through by slugs and snails: search them out and exterminate. Damage to dormant plants, young plants and young shoots in spring by slugs and snails: cover crown of plant with one inch thick layer of sharp sifted coal or coal ash during the winter. Soot gathered fresh from chimney and placed on soil surface around the plants in early spring will keep slugs and snails at bay.

GLADIOL (GLADIOLI)
Buds bored into and blooms eaten by caterpillars and small slugs: inspect plant daily and pick off pests. Bulbs of gladiol holed by wireworm: trap these pests as advised under CARROT.

HOLLYHOCKS
Foliage made unsightly by rusty spots. Cut off diseased leaves and burn. To prevent recurrence the following year: spray plants in March/April with Bordeaux mixture. Repeat when flower spikes begin to push.

MARIGOLDS

Foliage eaten by caterpillars: search for pests on underside of leaf. To discourage the egg-laying butterfly and moths: spray foliage above and below with quassia and soft soap solution. Repeat up to time of flowering.

NASTURTIUM

Greenfly and blackfly can quickly cripple and destroy the plants: Spray with pyrethrum solution and paraffin solution. Next day syringe with clean water.

PANSIES AND VIOLAS

These flowers can be affected by cuckoo spit. Within the spit there are yellow or pale green grubs draining the sap of the plant. Remove with piece of stick and destroy. Spray with paraffin emulsion.

ROSES

Greenfly: nicotine or pyrethrum solution for destruction of the greenfly. Nibbled flower buds: sacrifice the bud together with the small bug therein. Leaves showing white mildew: dust with sulphur when leaves and shoots are damp. Black spot: as a deterrent, spray with tar oil and also winter wash in the dormant season.

SWEET PEAS

Seedlings attacked by slugs. Young plants and surrounding soil should be dusted with *old* soot, or with dry wood ash. Young shoots and flower buds can be pecked by birds so bits of shiny tin or other metal suspended here and there on the plants will deter.

VIOLETS

Leaves distorted or look unhealthy because of minute red spider in droves on the underside. Spray underside leaves forcibly with nicotine solution. Water frequently with clear water because dry weather encourages these pests.

GREENHOUSE PLANTS IN GENERAL

Red spider, green fly, black and white fly, mites and thrips! Too dry conditions encourage these devils. There's always something isn't there?

7 MY GARDEN

The philosopher who said that work well done never needs doing over never weeded a garden.

Anon.

My garden has many weeds in it but it does also have flowers for most of the year. When my time comes to depart this life I would like flowers from my garden to accompany me on my last journey on earth. However, I must confess that there would be certain times when I should have to leave in a sort of Babes in the Wood situation.

In early January it is hard to find a flower in my garden but, before the month is midway through, snowdrops will be pushing their white drooping heads wondrously through the soil and they will stay pluckily to cheer me for six weeks or so, submitting to all kinds of weather.

February will see those game little snowdrops joined by clumps of crocuses in yellow and purple shadings. To see this mingling of colour at that particular time of year never fails to give me a special thrill. There is something really heartwarming about the early flowers. For instance their delight in multiplying and their love of remaining in the ground.

If you want a poor show of snowdrops take them up one year, dry them off and replant them in September. They will not enjoy the experience one little bit, even if you do. And they will show their displeasure the following spring by a display of sparse sulking droopy heads.

Come March and a sea of daffodils will breeze through the cool earth although this sometimes happens in February. My daffodils are closely followed by primroses, the polyanthuses and later the bluebells. Mine is a country garden on the outskirts of a small town.

After, and sometimes during the time of the bluebells, it will be the turn of the hyacinths, lilies of the valley and the grape hyacinths.

In early June my roses will begin to flower. Some years they flower from June until December although I have cut roses in January. I am a dab hand at pruning roses. I love it, as I leap around with the secateurs at the appropriate time, and sometimes at the inappropriate time.

In May and June the scent of purple lilac and white lilac fills my garden. When I moved in there were nine lilac bushes in my tiny garden. It was like a blooming forest of lilac, and there was no way my garden could continue to accommodate so many lilac bushes. So I attacked them regretfully but with vigour until I was down to one white double lilac and four purples, and I was bushed.

Honeysuckle and lavender make the summer morning air very attractive and encourage deep breathing. To stand in my garden and draw in great gulps of honeysuckle and lavender air is paradise to me.

Clumps of irises amid the strategically placed stones are a welcome sight until the blasted pests start making them all ragged. I must not forget to mention my palest of pink hollyhocks (ignoring the pest eaten lower leaves) and then there are the sturdy forget me nots with their strong blue flowers.

My tamarisk tree (a deciduous shrub) provides interest as its awl-shaped leaves change from a really pale to a medium shade of green; then almost grey. And in August the fragile pink feathery fronds make a pretty picture. And my rowan tree (mountain ash) is a constant source of delight.

October brings the cream plumes of the pampas grass while, if I am lucky (and I usually am), the roses and the chrysanthemums give colour.

In truth, towards the end of December there is little to be seen in my garden patch other than the plumes of the pampas grass, unless the high winds or the cats have knocked them down, or I might have used them for display — the pampas plumes not the cats.

Sometime during the year my South African cowslip (Elephant's Ears) and my Rose of Sharon colour the garden and all year round the darlings give ground cover which is a general deterrent to the weeds.

I do have a rockery. True, it simply comprises some half a dozen stones thrown casually on the ground. But I did the casual throwing and it is my very own rockery. Aubretia, snow-on-the-mountain, Cornish Pansies, Cornish Orchids, Dianthus (Carnation family) and Ice Plant (Echeveria) wander over and among the stones. There are tulips and daffodils along the top and also a miniature begonia down in the rockery itself. A couple of rose bushes form a backcloth.

I have had to rearrange the rockery somewhat as I did have some of the smaller plants obscured by the taller ones which proves what a fool I am.

Aubretia is a low growing hardy evergreen perennial with a purple flower. It does provide a bright show on dry walls and in my case adds to the colour in the rockery. It needs a sunny position and lime soil although mine thrives in clay soil...in the shade. Dianthus is the genus which includes the well known carnation, pink and sweet william; mine is a hardy dwarf species. It is perennial and is suitable for a rockery. Snow-on-the-moountain (Euphorbian Marbinata) has bright green leaves that become edged and veined. This low growing plant creeps all over the place and bits of it can be pulled out at random without any ill effects. It does not require any attention. I am rather partial to Snow-on-the-mountain.

A rockery can be a total joy. Both for humans and for slugs. Mine is a hot bed in which I do believe the slugs have veritable sex orgies. For truly they do multiply and sally forth.

8 THE HERB GARDEN

Borage drunk in wine makes men and women glad and merry, driving away all madness and dullness.

John Gerard, Elizabethan Herbalist.

Most herbs are none too particular about the type of soil they live in. This is a blessed relief. But, having said that most herbs do enjoy and thrive on a light, sandy well-drained soil in a sunny position. Mint and chives flourish in a shady bed. Rosemary and tarragon like the full sun.

April is the sowing time for savory, sage, fennel, thyme and parsley. At this time of year mint is increased by root division, chives should be divided into clumps of six bulbs; and mix wood ash with the soil for a happy band of chives; tarragon likes leaf mould in its little planting hole and thyme likes lime around it. Well, there would be some snags wouldn't there?

ANGELICA
Biennial; sow in April in deep rich soil.

ANISÉ
Annual; sow in May in light warm soil. The English summer is not usually warm enough for this herb so I don't know what you can do about that.

BASIL
Annual; sow in warm weather in March (you'll be lucky!) Failing that, sow in a warm sheltered position in April or May.

BAY
Perennial; plant in May in a sunny sheltered position.

BORAGE
Annual; sow in March and May in good soil in an open position.

CARAWAY
Biennial; sow in April or May but, just to confuse you, it won't flower until the following summer.

CHAMOMILE
Perennial; plant in autumn or spring in poor dry soil. Carefully store and dry the flower heads which should be picked as they open.

CHERVIL
Annual; sow in March, also in October for the Spring.

CHIVES
Perennial; plant bulbs in spring or autumn. Propagate by division and replanting each year.

DILL
Annual; sow in March in a warm border in light rich soil.

FENNEL
Perennial; sow in March. When established divide roots in the same season.

GARLIC
Annual, but propagate by dividing bulbs into cloves for use the following year. Plant cloves in autumn or early spring four inches apart in a sunny position.

HORSERADISH
Perennial; plant root (pieces of) in March. Horseradish is a prolific grower.

MARJORAM
Perennial; sow in a slight heat (in March), plant out in a warm sunny border, divide and transplant in autumn and spring.

Bay

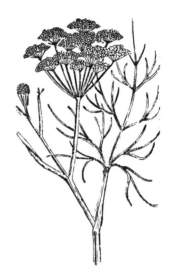

Fennel

Rosemary

Rue

MINT
Perennial; plant in February or March, re-plant (if well established) in fresh soil. It grows like a weed in my garden.

PARSLEY
Biennial; sow in February, again in May, again in July (it's never ending) if you want a good supply. Parsley likes free soil of good quality.

ROSEMARY
Perennial; likes a sheltered position and light dry soil. It is increased by cuttings or rooted slips taken off in spring.

RUE
Perennial; good tempered in ordinary garden soil; propagate by cuttings or slips and it will ripen and increase abundantly.

SAGE
Perennial; likes sunny position and good drainage. Increase by earthing up the outside stems. Can be taken off after a year as rooted plants in April and May.

TARRAGON
Perennial, likes light dryish soil. Increase by division in October or March. Transplant every year or two.

THYME
Perennial; plant in light dry warm soil, divide roots in April. Thyme is nice and happy in a rockery.

WORMWOOD
Perennial...will grow in any soil but is most aromatic in dry poor soil. Usually self-sown plants are found around the plant each autumn. The grey leaves of the wormwood are alleged to repel the cabbage butterfly. Dried leaves from wormwood are supposed to keep the moths away if placed in drawers.

Even a small garden can usually accommodate a herb garden.

9 THE SHRUB GARDEN

*Gardens are not made by singing 'Oh! How Beautiful'
and sitting in the shade.*

Rudyard Kipling

There is nothing as beautiful as a flower in a seed catalogue *unless* it is a shrub in a picture.

BROOM
Hardy perennial. Colour: brown to pale yellow tones. Can grow to eight feet tall and make a good windbreak. Long summer flowering. Plant throughout the summer and autumn. Propagation by seed or cuttings. Sow seeds in open in early autumn. It is possible to obtain seeds from the mother plant when it ceases flowering and the pods have appeared, so get to know someone who has a mother plant. Likes shade and sunshine.

BUDDLEIA
Hardy and half hardy perennial. Evergreen or deciduous depending on variety. Variety of colours. Flowering season is May to June. Great attraction to the butterflies. Height up to twenty feet but can be just three to four feet. Plant in flowering position in October or March in good loamy soil in full sun. They will tolerate lime. Propagation. Take nine to twelve inch cuttings in October and put in nursery bed outside. Plant in flowering position the following October. Pruning: in March, cut all the previous years' growth back to within two or three inches of the old wood. This produces strong erect stems and large clusters of flowers.

CAMELLIA
Hardy perennial, but some are half hardy. Loved for their glossy foliage and bowl-shaped flowers which can be single or double. Wide range of shades in pink, white and red. Height from three

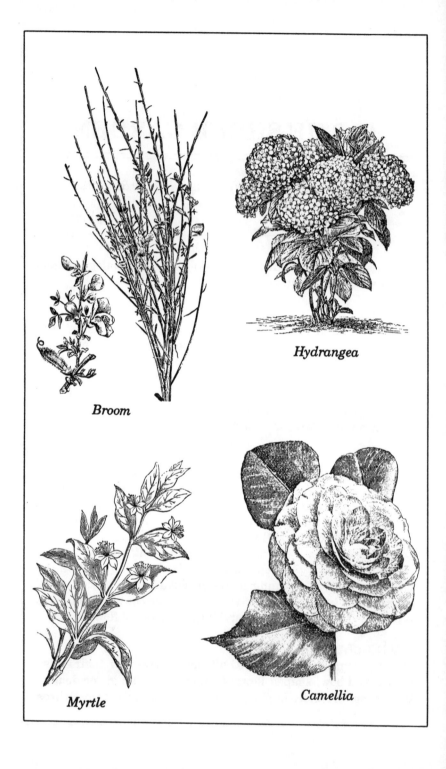

Broom

Hydrangea

Myrtle

Camellia

to twelve feet depending on variety. Flowers in late winter/ early spring. Needs a lime-free soil. Light soil should be enriched with leaf mould. Do not plant facing east. Likes protected westerly position. Windy and exposed conditions do not appeal to them — neither do they enjoy being waterlogged. Plant in September to October or March to April in flowering position. Give potash; do not prune. Propagate by taking cuttings from June to August using shoots or leaves.

CEANOTHUS
Hardy perennial. Variety of beautiful blues. Height can be from three feet to ten feet depending on variety. Flowers from July until autumn. Plant in September or April and May in sunny open position. They are not happy with a high lime content. Propagation by cuttings taken in July. Cut the deciduous variety back to the old wood in April.

FORSYTHIA
Hardy perennial. Varying shades of yellow flowers usually appear before the leaves. Height four to twelve feet. Flowers March to April. Plant from October to March in sun or partial shade. Flourishes in any aspect even an east or north facing wall. Propagation: take cuttings in October, should be ready for planting one year later. Prune as soon as flowering is over by removing old and damaged wood and shorten vigorous flowering shoots to keep the shrubs tidy. Can make a very attractive hedge.

HONEYSUCKLE
Hardy perennial. Beautiful fragrance. Colours are a mixture of pinks and reds and creams. Will grow from six feet to thirty feet. Flowers from June to September and sometimes later. Planting from September to October. Propagation: take four-inch long stem sections in July to August and insert them in peat and sand in a cold frame. Plant out rooted shrub cuttings in a nursery bed from April to May and then place in flowering position in September to October. Thin out old wood on outdoor plants occasionally after flowering.

HYDRANGEA
Hardy and half hardy perennial. Deciduous or evergreen. Variety

of colours commonly known as changeable because they can change their colour. Height can be up to six feet or more. Flowering season during the summer. Likes good loamy soil that is moisture retentive, and a sheltered position. Prepare soil with well decayed manure or compost or peat and plant in October to November or March to April. Propagation: take four to six inch cuttings from non-flowering shoots in August or September, and place in cold frame. Plant out in nursery rows the following April to May and plant into their final flowering position in autumn. Remove dead flower heads in March. Alkaline soils nearly always turn the blue varieties pink, and acid or neutral soils frequently turn pink varieties blue or purple.

LAVENDER
Hardy perennial. Unique perfume, purple flowers. Height eighteen inches to two or three feet. Flowers from May to July. Plant between September and March; for hedges set the young plants nine to twelve inches apart. Propagation: break off shoots and stick them in the ground. They should readily root. Remove dead flower stems in late summer and cut shrubs and trim hedges in March and April. Inclined to get leggy so best to replace every five or six years. The flowers can be dried to use in sachets or for pot pourri.

LILAC
Hardy perennial. Deciduous. Single and double blooms in white, pink or lilac. Fragrant. Height six to twelve feet. Flowers early May to late June. Plant in March in sunny position. Propagate by cuttings taken in July to August. Put in nursery bed until March for planting in flowering position two years later. It is supposed to be unlucky to take the beautiful blooms indoors.

MYRTLE
Half hardy perennial. Height up to ten feet. Fragrant white flowers appear from May until June. Needs sheltered sunny position. Plant in May in good well-drained soil. Propagation: take cuttings in June or July and put in heated greenhouse or hope for weather conditions of sixty degrees. Remove straggly shoots in late March.

PYRACANTHA (FIRETHORN)

Hardy perennial. Height up to ten feet. Tiny white flowers appear in June to July but give way to red or yellow berries which last from September until March. Plant from October onwards. Thrives in any position. Propagation: softwood cuttings taken in July or August should be rooted in a greenhouse under frost-free conditions. Or ,hardwood cuttings in October can be planted in a cold frame. Or gather the berries when they are ripe in October and squash them to reach the seeds and sow those seeds in a cold frame in October.

VIBURNUM (GUELDER ROSE)

Hardy perennial. Deciduous and evergreen depending on variety. Height up to fifteen feet. Fragrant summer flowering. Will thrive in any good moist soil. Best grown in the full sun. Evergreen variety should be planted in September to October or March to May. Deciduous species from October to March. Propagation: cuttings with a heel in September can be rooted in a cold frame. Put in nursery bed for two to three years before planting in flowering position. Also seeds can be sown in September or October in a cold frame but germination could take eighteen months and then growth is slow. Most species take four to six years to reach flowering size. Pruning: thin out old and damaged wood of evergreen species in early May. Deciduous species require no special pruning, except to thin out overgrown shrubs and remove dead wood after flowering.

10 THE 'VEGGIE' PATCH

Let onion lurk within the bowl,
And, scarce suspected, animate the whole

Recipe for Salad: Rev. Sydney Smith:, 1771-1845

BEETROOT

Sow March, April, May, June for successive harvest through summer to autumn. Lift beetroot by carefully wriggling the spade. Twist off tops. Store in single layers. Use sifted ashes or sifted soil between each layer. Finish off with three inch deep layer of ashes: then 3 inch layer of dry straw. Plonk a twist of straw right down through the top six inches of the 'pyramid'. We always store our beetroot like this in a dry frost-proof shed. Turnips can be stored the same way.

BRUSSELS SPROUTS

Sow March and April for winter harvest. Gathering: cut from plant with a sharp knife. Work your way up the stem cutting the lower ones first. Cut the top leaves off and use. This will cause the sprouts to swell. My mum always said that sprouts cut after a hard frost tasted finest.

CABBAGE

Sow spring for autumn/winter harvest. Sow July/August for spring harvest. Cut when firm and also solid but leave a few of the outer leaves. Cut an X on the top of a cabbage stump after you have cut the cabbage and, with luck, you'll grow some extra greens on that stump. If you want to put heart into a spindly cabbage make a vertical cut in the stem and wedge the cut open with a piece of stick. It sound very cruel, but it usually works.

LETTUCE
Sow out of doors from February/March to August for continuous supply. When you lift lettuce for transplanting take all the roots. If you break the roots you could have bolting lettuce. Also make the hole deep enough to take the length of the roots. It is not easy gardening. You have to keep your wits about you. (Lettuce at night is supposed to relax you. No, not planting it)

PURCHASING ONION BULBS
If you must purchase onion bulbs/seedlings, and why not, they should have plenty of longish roots and not have yellow leaves. Again you will be needing the rich firm soil. Plant the bulbs/ seedlings approximately six inches apart in rows six inches apart in March or April. See that half their depth only is covered in soil and remains so. They need to be able to expand. Water often. You have no choice but to weed close to the bulbs by hand. They do not take kindly to the soil near them being disturbed and a hoe could do irreparable damage. Once a week throw some poultry manure between the rows followed by a good dosing of water. Discontinue the manuring at the end of July.

Try to avoid letting the plants run to seed unless it is onion seed you are seeking. If a thick central stem starts rearing its head nip it in the bud. In other words cut it right out. And use that onion before it starts messing about again. In a really wet summer — like most summers — the foliage at the base of the tops can be almost as thick as the bulb. Try bending the tops over as soon as possible but even so these onions will be of scant use for storage.

To accelerate ripening, scrape the soil away from around the bulbs with the back of a Dutch hoe. When the tops start browning, ripening is further accelerated by bending all the tops over. Don't put up with any messing about with the tops that come back up. Get them down. The point of bending the tops is that the upward flow of sap is stopped and within a couple of days you can start lifting. The bulbs should come out of the ground easily. Loosen the soil alongside the rows, grab the tops and just pull.

Dry off by exposing to the sun by lying them out on a hard path or dry wood or dry ground. If it's raining they will have to be dried under cover. Do not store until the onions are perfectly dry and don't store any bruised ones in any event. Do not store them in a sack or deep box. If you haven't sufficient floor space tie them with string by the necks, a bit like the French onion sellers use to do. Onions, like women, thrive best with loving care and attention.

ONIONS SOWN FROM SEED (NOT BULBS OR SEEDLINGS)

The soil must be prepared carefully, unless you are using soil that has already had a good digging — perhaps a good deep digging for a crop of carrots or peas or even cabbage. The soil should have been dug to a depth of two feet with animal manure or the remains of decaying cabbage patch worked in for good measure. And worked in at depth. Roll the ground but as this should be in a sunny position this should not be too unpleasant. If you haven't a roller you will just have to tread it. If after all this attention the ground is still not firm fork or rake the surface while working in plenty of wood ash and soot.

Sow seed in early March. Sow as thinly as possible in little trenches (shallow trench the width of a spade) about one foot apart and three quarters of an inch deep. Drop three or four seeds together at intervals of approximately six inches. As soon as required thin out the onions so that they are about half an inch apart. Remember, at the second and later thinnings it will be possible for you to use those pulled out efforts as spring onions. You can sow seed under glass in a sunny position if you wish in mid-February. Prepare a shallow box, or a pot if you wish, with two thirds good soil, one third well sifted leaf mould, then sprinkle some sharp grit or sifted sand. Firm the soil. It is no good treading it in: you could break the box.

Sow seed thinly and cover thinly with sifted soil. When the plants are about three inches high plant them one and a half inches apart. Very gradually harden these plants off by exposing them to cooler conditions for planting out in April or early May. Plant them in rows one foot apart at intervals of four to six inches. Or again you can plant them just two inches apart if you want to provide yourself with the opportunity to pull spring onions. Remember those that are left to grow bigger should be four to six inches apart. NB: Each young plant should be placed in a hole quite deep enough to take the root's full length. When the hole is filled in make sure only a *tiny part* of the bulb should be *below the surface*.

The tops will topple over to begin with and may be nibbled at by garden friend or foe. If this happens just snip the tips off so that the root hold can be maintained. They will not be happy if the roots are out of the ground and neither will you. Water all newly planted onion plants.

TURNIPS

Dig ground one foot deep and throw in rotted greenstuff or old manure. Bury this about seven to eight inches down. Sow half an inch deep in rows nine inches apart. Make sure the soil is dry for sowing and sow thinly. Turnips are nitrogen fixing plants and so are very useful to the soil. So are beans and peas. To benefit the soil do as follows: after picking beans and peas the haulms (tops to the uninitiated) of the plants should be cut off and put on the compost heap. But the roots should remain in the ground because of their nitrogenous value.

TOMATOES

You can grow these from seed or buy plants. The best plants are those which are short jointed with really dark green leaves. So if you've grown from seed and the plants don't match up to the description in the previous sentence scrub your plants and go out and buy some.

Outdoor tomatoes like the sun. Sow the little seeds in a mixture of peat and sand in a pot and put in the kitchen window — light and warmth are essential. As soon as the first leaf is formed put them in individual pots or seed box with a similar mixture. Put in cold frame to harden off. Meanwhile prepare their next home by digging the proposed site to eighteen inch depth. Work in leaf mould or hop manure nine inches down with plenty of wood ash mixed in with the top soil. I would not advocate stable manure at this stage. Late May or early June the plants can be moved into the prepared site. For at least one hour before planting soak with water. As you remove the plants from the pots make sure that the roots are disturbed as little as possible.

Plant eighteen inches apart. Make hole for plant large enough to take the roots plus soil comfortably. Sink the empty pot down in the ground *by* the plant and *water via this pot*. This ensures that the moisture reaches the roots and a crust will not form around the plant. In the event of the possibility of a frost, cover plants with paper hats made with newspaper or similar. Remove the covering during the day. At the time of planting stakes should be driven in. They should be roughly three inches behind the plant and about five feet high. Loosely tie each plant to its own stake with raffia or string. Constantly remove side shoots which appear at leaf joints so that single stems remain.

Water frequently during dry spells. When the bottom truss of fruit is formed feed with liquid manure. Regular weekly feeds from then on. After the fourth truss is formed the top of the plant should be pinched out. Fruit should be gathered individually as it ripens. If cracks appear in the tomatoes you haven't watered them efficiently. You've let them dry out and then watered. This will not do. Regular watering is essential in dry periods and for greenhouse tomatoes regular watering is essential. If you need to increase the amount of water do so gradually for if you double up greenhouse tomatoes will grow with shock splits.

POTATOES

Odd that 'Pomme de Terre' should be the French for potato when the advice is 'never plant potatoes near apple trees.' Maybe it's different in France!

There is nothing difficult about growing potatoes — apart from the backache. To achieve a really good crop it is essential to obtain good planting tubers. It is possible to estimate roughly the amount you will crop from a certain quantity of seed potatoes. For example, 240 feet, say eight rows of thirty feet, should produce four hundredweight.

It is perhaps advisable to plant a row of an early variety such as Arran Pilot or Homeguard. Second crop varieties include Foremost and Ben Lomond; main crop varieties are Desirée, King Edward, Majestic and Arran Banner. Size of the seed potatoes is of the utmost importance — those the size of a hen's egg are favourite. If you have seed from your own crop, they should be selected from the crop when it is being lifted in its entirety. This is important because the seed potatoes should be picked from those plants which have produced an abundant crop.

The soil must be broken up quite finely and to as great a depth as possible. Potatoes won't grow in lumpy soil. Bury manure about nine inches down — too deep, for the seed potatoes, when planted, to touch. Compost, seaweed or *old* manure are all suitable. The growing begins from the eye of the tuber. The best eyes form at the broad end. They need to sprout roughly half an inch before planting. To start the sprouting place the seed potatoes touhing each other, in shallow boxes, wide end at the top. *Put only one layer in each box.* Place boxes in frost-free building; if you have nowhere then cover the boxes with paper or straw but remove that as soon as there is no danger of frost. Seed potatoes need careful handling as they bruise easily and this can cause rot.

Do not water. It is light they require, not moisture. Limit the indivudual sprouts to one, or two at the most, strong-looking individuals at the wide end. Larger than hen-sized tubers can be allowed two sprouts and cut in two before planting — let those cut harden off. The ready-cut tubers should be planted in warm ground from late February to the middle of May. If it's cold and wet, wait awhile. All the varieties, whether very early, early or main crop can, if necessary, be planted at the same time. They will be ready for lifting when they have each completed their growth cycle. But, if possible, it is best to plant the first cropping variety in February.

Plant early tubers about a foot apart; rows should be two feet apart and aligned north/south if possible so both sides get the sun when the plants appear. Bury four inches deep in heavy soil; six inches in light soil. Carry the tubers in their single layer boxes to planting area. Keep soil loose between rows by hoeing. This will keep the weeds under control. Do not disturb the soil too close to the planting line. Earth up the potato plants when the leaves appear by drawing the soil with a hoe and piling against the leaves without covering the leaves. This will serve to keep the developing potatoes in the dark. Without these mounds they go slightly green and are bitter to the taste. The first earthing should take place when leaves are approximately six inches high. When they are a foot high earth up again making a continuous bank of soil with sloping sides and the leaves at the top sitting in a little V-shaped depression. This V-shape holds rain to feed the thirsty roots. To earth up, straddle the row, walk backwards carefully, hoe on rightside and left, alternately holding the draw hoe at an angle of 45 degrees. Potato plants are not hardy and frost can upset them.

Lift earlies when tops begin to yellow. Lift one plant only first to check if the potato skin is tough: if so, this is a sure sign that they are ready. The later varieties are ready for lifting when the green foliage has faded or even died down.

Spider

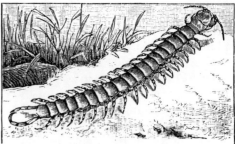

Centipede

Ladybird

Garden Friends

Woodlouse

Garden Enemies

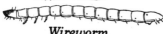

Wireworm

Slug

Earwig

11 GARDEN PESTS

(If you haven't a strong stomach you should skip this chapter)

Any thing or person that is noxious, destructive or troublesome; a bane, curse, plague.

The Shorter Oxford Dictionary

APHIS (APHIDS)
Plants look unhealthy, leaves curl and wither, and millions of these ghastly aphids are clinging together. They really do congregate in their thousands. And they cause the dreaded blight, not to mention death. Fling lukewarm soapy water over the affected parts, then wash off with clean water for the aphis is as keen on soapy water and being clean as little boys. So the soap and water method should help to get rid of aphids. Spray with nicotine for they do not like tobacco smoke either. In the dormant season spray with tar oil. Beetles, spiders and lady birds eat aphids, as do birds. Nettles in the garden should attract aphids and greenfly away from other plants.

CABBAGE GRUBS
Cabbage grubs attack the cabbage, broccoli and cauliflower roots: plants droop and die. Prevent this happening by mixing slaked lime, soot and earth (one part lime, one part soot, three parts earth) and plonk in hole before putting plant in the ground. The herb wormwood (*see* section on HERBS) is alleged to repel the cabbage butterfly. However, if the worse comes to the worse run around the cabbage patch picking the caterpillars off the lovely cabbages and kill them (ugh!). Tobacco water can be useful: throw it around.

EAR-WIGS
They like the shade and dahlias. Place a stake at the side of the

dahlia and put an inverted flower pot on it, preferably with some crumpled newspaper inside. The ear-wigs will seek out the shade in the pot and all you have to do is kill them.

MILLIPEDES

A potato buried in the soil will attract them. Put a slice of carrot or potato on a stick just below the surface of the ground and examine daily.

SNAILS AND SLUGS

Arm yourself with a light in the dark nights, and a bucket of strong salty water, sally forth and sling those slugs in the bucket. A thick layer of soot around your plants will protect them from these fat greedy fellows. The white side of orange peel will attract slugs and snails for easy gathering. Hedgehogs eat slugs — adopt a hedgehog! A dish of beer will attract slugs. Use equal portions of beer and water, stir in a bit of brown sugar and cover dish. At least you know they will die jolly.

CABBAGE WHITE BUTTERFLY

I should have said this comes from a caterpillar which is fat and yellow with dark spots. Hand pick off or spray with saline solution (one tablespoon of salt to one gallon of water). *See* CABBAGE GRUBS. Mothballs placed in cleft sticks among the spring cabbage should help to keep the butterflies away.

WOOD LICE AND WIREWORM

Trap by planting hollow pieces of apple or potato, etc. Put the slices of potato or apple or carrot speared with a stick just two inches below the soil surface. Again you will have to examine daily and destroy your catch. (Remember to mark the sticks. Remember those happy carefree days before you had a garden?)

CARROT FLY

They can do a lot of damage to carrots but they are not very good flyers. Put a two feet high netting mesh around the carrot patch and you will ground the carrot fly.

WOOD LICE

Put down old rotting board and flat stones, they find them

attractive hiding places — then exterminate those hidden tenants.

CENTIPEDES & BLACK BEETLES, SPIDERS, LADYBIRDS AND MONEY SPIDERS

These are the gardener's friends. (He has so few). These friends feed on damaging insects. The big snag is that it is easy to muddle centipedes with other pests and kill off some of them. They *are* something like the millepede which are root-eating pests which coil up when disturbed. But black beetles are easily identifiable and they feed on slugs (yippee!) Apart from centipedes your best friends are soapy water, soot and ashes.

SPECIFIC ENEMIES OF THE VEGGIES

BROADBEANS

Black fly: treat with paraffin emulsion. Black fly spreads downwards so try pinching out the tips of the plants and burning them. Then spray with the paraffin emulsion.

BEET AND CELERY

Leaves tunnelled by grubs (the leaf mining fly): pick off leaves or crush grubs to death between fingernail and thumb. To discourage: attack in the spring with quassi and soft soap solution. Black fly on leaves: spray with nicotine or pyrethrum solution (they both come in powder or liquid form). Weevils will damage broadbean seedlings; old soot or derris powder scattered over foliage should do the trick.

DWARF FRENCH RUNNER BEANS

Prone to black fly....get to it with the nicotine or pyrethrum in powder or liquid form. Yellowish patches on seedlings and pods. Destroy immediately the affected plants to check disease. Pale spotted foliage due to minute red spiders, worse in long dry weather: spray each evening with clear water.

CABBAGE TRIBE

Greenfly on leaves: counteract with derris powder or pyrethrum or salt solution. Seedlings nibbled by turnip fly....dust with old soot or derris or nicotine powder. Swellings (or galls) at base of stem on cabbage tribe and on turnips. Reject young plants showing these swellings which contain the rotten old weevil grub. Change venue for next year. Cabbage tribe (eg. savoy, cauliflower, brussels sprouts, etc. 'club root disease' or in turnip known as 'finger and toe')! Root disease: do not use site for cabbage tribe for 3 or 4 years. Lime soil before planting next time. Cabbage root fly causes plants to wilt: pull up and burn attacked plants. Cabbage white fly is deterred if you plant marigolds along rows.

CARROTS
Roots eaten by grubs of carrot fly. To prevent this, put fresh soot around the plant or paraffin tainted sand or sifted fire ash.

CELERY
See also BEETS. Rusty spots spreading over foliage: spray with bordeaux mixture as preventative, destroy really mangy plants.

LETTUCE
Greenfly: spray immediately with pyrethrum solution. Small holes in leaves: change site for next lettuce crop. Stems rotting at soil level (grey mould disease): destroy affected plants immediately. Grow next crop elsewhere.

ONION
White flugg mould (white rot disease) at base of bulbs. Remove and burn plants. Young plants yellow and wilting means grubs! Spray early with paraffin emulsion. Pull up and burn the worst. Shrivelled foliage (mould). Dust early and well with flowers of sulphur when foliage wet with dew or rain. Swollen stems — eelworm: no remedy, so do not grow on same bed.

PARSNIP
Grub tunnelling inside leaves: *see* BEET. Weevil: *see* BROAD-BEANS. Greenfly: spray with nicotine and pyrethrum solution.

POTATO
Potato blight: brown blotches on leaves, also on tubers: spray with Bordeaux mixture in early June, then again three weeks later.

Tuber scabbed but fit to eat! Scab disease: ground not to be limed but in soil of gritty nature line drills with leaf mould, or sprinkle flowers of sulphur in drills.

COLORADO BEETLE (half an inch long and striped)
Its bright pink or red grubs on leaves. Notify local police immediately. Do not spray, await instructions. My grandfather was always looking for these but never found one.

TOMATOES
Green and black spots on foliage which dies and rolls up. Spray with Bordeaux mixture. Burn badly affected plants. Brown blotches on leaves (like potato blight) spray with Bordeaux mixture early *not* when toms ripening. White fly: grow marigolds close by as a deterrent, especially in the greenhouse. Root knot disease, indicated by foliage drooping and yellowing, stem limp, plant collapses (minute eelworm is the cause): uproot and burn plants and treat soil with quicklime before use again. Sleeping disease causes leaves to droop and mildew appears in lower parts of stem. Uproot plants, burn, treat soil with quicklime before using again. Canker of stem starts as gummy moist patches which become hard and dark and then whiten: uproot and burn plants. Treat soil with quicklime before using again.

Black spot on fruit: destroy (black stripes attack stem low down and work upwards). Various forms of leaf rust can be troublesome — leaves can roll up and die. In the early stages prevent spreading to healthy leaves by dusting unaffected leaves with flowers of sulphur and picking off affected leaves and burning. Keep the greenhouse reasonably dry yet with plenty of air, ample space between plants and all the light possible.

Outdoor tomatoes may suffer blight (like potato blight): spray with Bordeaux mixture but not when fruit is ripening. Erratic watering can cause tomatooes to split and/or be mishapen. Tomatoes are creatures of steady habits.

IN GENERAL
Soot and other powders applied to soil with be ineffective when ground is wet with rain. Use fresh soot as a soil insecticide for application to soil only — not on plants. Will help to drive away the pests that are below the surface and also scare away egg laying

flies.

Dusting with powder: small bellows or other puffing device with container attached are useful. The medicine/poison in powder form can be shaken out of a small muslin bag, jerked about over plants or soil. You could attach the bag to a piece of stick then it is not close to you. Choose a dull day or calm evening otherwise there could be wastage by wind and do not even consider scattering if rain looks imminent.

Paraffin tainted sand or sifted fire ashes will scare away flies seeking to deposit eggs at the base of carrot, cabbage or other stems. Mixture spread around and alongside plants to be protected. Whatever is used you cannot expect to effect an immediate cure. You have to repeat as necessary and apply regularly. It is no use kidding yourself that by doubling the amount you can cure the problem at one go!

12 PROPAGATION and PRUNING

From fairest creatures we desire increase that thereby beauty's rose might never die.

William Shakespeare

PROPAGATION

BUDDING
Standard roses can be increased by budding. This is not as complicated as it sounds. Transfer a dormant leaf bud (not a flower bud), taken from any standard to the stem or shoot of a briar. The idea is to persuade the dormant leaf bud to grow in the briar's own tissues. This should be carried out around July to August. When the bud has definitely taken, make absolutely certain that the briar's own leaf growth is allowed below or above the bud. The briar will then turn into the rose variety from which the bud was taken. Talk about cuckoo in the nest.

DIVISION OF ROOTS
This is a good way of increasing plants of a perennial nature. It is a splendid way of accumulating stock for the herbaceous border. The plan is to take a plant clump to pieces and planting each piece which is complete with root or roots separately. Some herbaceous plants such as phlox will produce a tough root mass which will have to be levered apart with a trowel or fork. Usually it is wise to plant the younger, outer pieces in good soil and dump the older worn out centre. Irises of the flag variety have to be brought out of the ground with a fork and the root cut through where division is selected on the brittle root stocks.

Autumn and early spring are good times for this kind of division. Dahlias are good subjects for division. Take them from the winter store in spring and pack them in broken leaf mould or lightish soil, but be sure they are covered. In their boxes they should be placed in a cold frame a greenhouse. Several shoots will appear from each clump with a bit of luck and you can separate each single tuber from it's former stem and pot it in rich soil to grow. I have obtained five or six new dahlia plants from one old clump by this method using the cold frame.

STEM CUTTINGS

It is possible to increase your stock of all kinds of plants from shrubs to bedding plants by stem cutting. Select a stem and then cut through cleanly immediately below a joint. The rooting soil should have the appearance of a good compost with silver sand and leaf mould. Make sure you plant the cuttings in flower pots which are crocked for drainage or in boxes that have plenty of holes in the bottom. Water gently with a watering can with a rose on it. Then water as soil dictates. If the cuttings are in a garden frame try to keep out direct sunlight for a few weeks.

Remember not to have the ends of the cuttings ragged and it is best to cut off the lowest leaves. If you get fed up with this remember you are saving money. NB: rose or shrub cuttings should be about a foot long and should be planted in the open in half their depth with sand or grit at the bottom of the hole. Tread that soil quite firmly. Standard roses cannot be increased in this way. They are special: they have to be budded.

LAYERING

This is a delicate operation. Many shrubs, bush and rambler roses and carnations can be increased by this method. You have to make a nick with a knife through the shoot as close to the bottom of the plant as possible or at a suitable point where the shoot can be directed towards the soil. Then cover the cut section with two inches of soil. Be careful that the shoot is prevented from movement and it should be kept well watered until it has taken root. It can then be severed from its parent plant, lifted with its roots which, if all has gone according to plant, should have been produced from the area where the cut was made, and transferred to the spot where you wished it to flower. In the case of the carnation it is wisest to select shoots which have not flowered. Sometimes it is necessary to secure the shoot by wire. That will stop it trying to jump out of the ground until you are ready.

PIPING

This is the way to increase your stock of pinks and carnations although for carnations I prefer layering. Select a shoot which has not flowered, from a good plant, with one hand holding the main plant, so that you do not pull it out by mistake. Yank out the shoot. You need shoots around three to four inches long. The time for doing this is June or July. Pop them about two inches apart around the rim of small pots in a cold frame or they could go straight into the bed of the frame. Water them in and keep the frame closed for several weeks and gently shaded. My grandfather always used old newspapers. Accustom them slowly to the air and then plant them out in the autumn.

BULBS

Many bulbous plants make their own little bulbs. Plant these tiny bulbs about an inch deep in well drained soil. Keep watering them when they start pushing through.

PRUNING

The actual operation of pruning consists of removing parts of mainly woody plants, trees and shrubs. This does include roses. The point of removing stems, branches or roots is to divert the energy of the plant for a certain purpose. It will certainly divert your energy.

Principal reasons for pruning: to keep plant healthy, to keep plant well balanced; to make sure the plant is evenly shaped, to encourage the beauty of flower or foliage, characteristic shape or outline or whatever. Not all shrubs need regular annual pruning, and you can save yourself time and trouble by checking before planting the eventual size and shape of the tree or shrub and allowing ample room for growth. Bear in mind that over crowded trees and shrubs will require drastic pruning every year, otherwise they will become weak and out of shape as they struggle for root space, food, water and light. In other words, they need space the same as humans do. If you are seeking a healthy, vigorous plant you have no choice, but to grant it sufficient space and to prune correctly as required. For the longer dead wood is allowed to stay with a plant, the greater the risk of disease spores entering it, multiplying as in cancerous cells and spreading to healthy tissue. A plant, like a person, can die from disease if unattended. NB: Branches rubbing against each other can cause damage so should be cut away. Be drastic and strong minded. Thin, weak growths are of little or no use, particularly if they are in the centre of a bush where they would be starved of light and air. Keep the centre of that bush or shrub open so that air and light can circulate quite freely.

Make all pruning cuts cleanly, leaving no ragged edges or torn bark. Do not bruise or crush the stems as this could cause the tissues to die. Make the cut almost horizontally across a branch as this will speed up healing. Remember you are doctoring the tree or shrub. In the early days a young tree or shrub should be trained and pruned hard to get it into the correct or desired shape. Completely remove weak shoots, cut back side shoots to a facing bud on one or two year old growths. Remember, the buds are the only points from which further growth can develop along a stem, so prune as close as possible to a bud, making the cut on the side opposite the bud and finishing immediately above it. Once the framework of the tree or shrub has been established, careful pruning to maintain the shape is done by shortening, as necessary, one-year-old shoots back to a bud. Cut back thin or unwanted shoots and dead or damaged shoots flush with the main stem from which they arise.

The shaping of your tree or your shrub is entirely in your hands. It is up to you.

HYDRANGEAS (PRUNING)
I leave my hydrangea flowers clinging to its old stems until March or April. This provides frost protection. In the spring I cut the old stems back to base so that the new one year old stems can carry new growth.

WINTER SPRAYING OF FRUIT TREES AFTER PRUNING
Lime wash around the trunk or spray with tar oil wash, but only do this when buds are dormant, probably between early Decem-

ber and the middle of January. Most effective is a forceful spray so use a coarse nozzle to make sure you reach all those nasty little crevices. An old stirrup pump makes a good apparatus for doing this job. Old clothes, a hat (cap style) pulled down to protect eyes; and gloves of the gauntlet type should be worn for protection. Cover any plants or vegetables near the trees with sacking or newspaper. If any liquid hits a plant, hose down with water immediately. It is as well to strain the solution through coarse muslin before starting spraying. This keeps the nozzle clear and makes the job easier. Clean the apparatus and dry it after use (this is very boring but saves swearing later).

13 GARDENING CALENDAR

*To really enjoy garden work, put on a hat and gloves,
hold a little trowel in one hand — and tell the man
where to dig.*

Anon.

JANUARY

Burn all garden rubbish. Remember the utility area? Loosen soil
around any visible bulbs but do not go searching for them. Make
rock gardens. Wheel out the manure and the compost during the
frosty weather. Sow lettuce, endive and parsley in cold frames if
you have them. Plant shallots in a warm border.

If any bulbs such as narcissus, anemone or tulips have not yet
been planted get them in during the first spell of decent weather,
otherwise you could be too late. Any which were planted earlier
and are putting in an appearance should be protected from frost
and heavy rain by scattering fern or soft straw over them.

Prune bush fruits and trees by cutting out all dead wood. It is
best to keep the centre of the bushes open so that they can have
plenty of air; cut back side shoots (but not the natural fruit spurs)
to three or four buds, making the cut just above a bud that is
pointing outwards. Choose mild weather. Spray fruit trees and
bushes with tar-oil wash. Dig up rhubarb roots and divide.

Start thinking about your vegetable plot and you might go as
far as getting your seed potatoes. Sow onions, tomatoes and

lettuce under glass in seed boxes. Have a look in the shed at the dahlia tubers and if they are looking a bit damp, take them into a warm dry place and stay with them.

Plant fruit trees if weather reasonable (is it ever?) although in truth it would have been better to have done this in the autumn. Better put some mulching over the roots to protect them from frost and from draught which could occur in the spring unless we have torrential rain as usual. Fork around flower beds and borders if you are looking for something to do.

FEBRUARY

Sprinkle soot around polyanthuses and forget-me-nots. If the weather isn't too ghastly spike lawn with fork, rake and apply lime. Rake over the beds and borders regularly. After frost check to see if any of the plants have been raised. If they have push them back in again. That should give them the general idea. Give the roses a good mulching with dung.

Now is the time when the mice could make for the crocuses and the tulips so if you see a mousehole fill it up with soot. Look at strawberry beds and watch out for canker on fruit bushes.

Sow lettuce, onions, leeks and parsley if you did not get around to it last month. Sow parsnips. You should now be sowing lettuce at fortnightly intervals until Midsummers Day. Move little plants to three inches apart as soon as possible, then twelve inches. If you have a rich but light soil your lettuce will like you. After all that sowing you may not like them! Prune apricots, peaches, nectarines and plums in between sowing all those lettuce. If you must sow hardy annuals you may as well get on with doing it towards the end of the month.

Cut back pampas grass and burn out dead leaves.

MARCH

Crocuses should be in full bloom with hyacinths, tulips, etc., adding to the glory. Roll the grass, remove daisies and dandelions from the lawn with small fork and brute force if you are fanatical enough to want a green sward for a lawn. Sow seed or the little tufts of grass you have removed from the borders in the bare patches thus exposed. Fork the borders ever so gently.

Finish pruning apples, pears, cherries, gooseberries and currants. Be sure to finish rose pruning by mid-March, but make this pruning quite drastic. Put out cinders to protect young shoots from those greedy slugs. Slugs will eat everything young and green given half a chance. Overhaul the rock garden. Yank out everything of which you have too much.

If you are going to sow hardy annuals and you did not get around to it last month, do it now.

Plant out seedling onions and also the onion sets. Onions grown from seed last summer should be planted a couple to three inches below the ground and six to nine inches apart. Kill wasps assiduously the second you spot them. Fork around the strawberries and mulch; use farmyard manure or compost.

Mushrooms: make ridges of built up dung (horse dung) brought fresh from the stables, also put down a layer of earth. After about ten days when the dung is not quite so hot take pieces of spawn bricks (purchased from the nursery) and insert in the mixture about a foot apart, mould over and press down with your feet. Pretend you're treading grapes, it is more romantic, hit with a spade if you're still conscious, water and press down again. Mushrooms should appear within a month or so — they'll be glad to jump out of that lot.

A reminder on rose pruning: remove dead wood. Cut down to a point above an outward pointing bud. Strong shoots can have six or seven buds below but weaker shoots need be left with only three buds or even four. Roses which were planted last November should now be looking quite lively and vigorous. After pruning the manure should be forked into the surface of the soil; it will give splendid mulch and protection from summer drought. Towards the end of March, on established roses, spread a layer of well decayed farmyard manure around the stems of the roses.

Cut down the lavender and the pampas grass if you haven't already.

APRIL

Get the hanging baskets sorted out. Line them with live moss. I usually collect mine on Dartmoor. Arrange the plants so that the drooping ones are hanging out over the side, otherwise the whole object is defeated. Hanging fuschia, lobelia and geraniums (the ivy-leafed variety), petunias, dwarf begonias and nasturtiums, but not altogether. The moss needs to be lined with potting compost. You don't have to drench yourself with water every time you water the hanging baskets. Just stand on tiptoe and put a whole load of ice cubes in approximately once a week or as necessary. Mulch all the newly planted fruit trees and water them wildly in dry weather.

Clip evergreens and prune flowering shrubs. This is also a good time to plant and mulch evergreen shrubs. Plant clematis against a north or west wall. This is also the time for planting out sweet peas, pansies, and carnations. At the first sign of greenfly start flinging soapy water over the roses. Feed the lilies of the valley with weak soot water. Sow parsley again. Lift and divide mint and chives. Overhaul the confounded herb garden.

This is the time when grafting takes place. Take up the daffodil bulbs at the end of April if you wish and store them in a dry place against September planting. I don't lift mine.

MAY

Keep a watchful eye on everything. This can be a treacherous month. Take up tulips if you like and store in the same manner as daffodil bulbs. Get rid of rose suckers by digging soil away and making a clean cut. Mulch and disbud roses. Look out for the frost and cover young seedlings with brown paper or fronds of bracken. Fork over dahlia sites and incorporate wood ashes. Remove suckers from raspberries. Divide rockery plants when blooms have faded. Have a happy time picking off the caterpillars from the gooseberries. Give well trained fruit trees a thorough soaking with water followed by a generous manure mulch. Dust strawberry plants with old soot. Look out for woolly aphis.... and drown them in soapy water. Plant out leeks. Hoe freely and merrily in your veggie garden. That is to say, hoe merrily between the crops if you have any. But *hand weed* the onion area.

Early May is usually a good time to plant early flowering chrysanthemums — they should bloom from September until November. Plant out the geraniums ,the fuchsias and the begonias now if you believe the frosts are over. Mow the confounded lawn.

JUNE

Protect plants from high winds by staking. Prune early blossoming shrubs such as lilac, and uproot suckers from the base of lilac. Restrict sweet peas to one or two stems, cut off dead blooms, old stems and seed pods. Keep hoe going in dry weather. If you wish, rid the lawn of daisies. Remove strawberry runners. Kill the ants. Sow swedes, main crop carrots and beet.

Distinguish between friends and foes in the garden. Don't forget that the centipede, ladybird, spider, frog and lizard, not to mention the earthworm, are all good friends. Not so the cabbage root fly, the cabbage white butterfly or the wireworm. Train hedges and mow the flipping lawns again. June is the month of the beautiful rose but if you haven't any in your garden it is too late to plant them. You will just have to watch out for roses in others people's gardens and plant some of your own in the autumn. At least you won't have to worry about keeping the roots moist, preferably with liquid manure. If you have roses watch out for the dreaded greenfly. Using a can with a rose (not the flower) on the end, spray with clean water, holding the leaf, and moving the fingers as you do so. It is very effective.

Trim edges of lawns, reversing edges as necessary. If you have a glorious bed of geraniums you should remember to remove spent flowers or they will run to seed.

Watch out for mildew on the roses. Lightly dust the stems and foliage with powdered sulphur and then water roots gently and later wildly.

Keep hoeing or hand forking to stir up the surface of the soil here, there and everywhere.

Pot chrysanthemums, stake securely and sink in bed of ashes in the shade (the chrysanthemums not you!)

Plant out the dahlias provided you are fairly sure the frosts are over. And even if you are not sure you'd best get them out now or you will be too late. Beware of letting violas, petunias, pansies or fuschias run to seed for it will depress the plants to such a state as to cause them to wither away to the rubbish dump. So cut the flowers in time to enjoy them in a vase. If there is heavy rain you will gain respite from watering *but*, if warm or even hot sunshine should follow and cause the soil to cake, nip out smartly with the hoe and fork and loosen the soil otherwise when the next shower comes the thirsty roots will remain thirsty.

Half way through, or perhaps even towards the end of the month, remove lower buds of dahlias to try to ensure larger blooms. It's at this season of the year that our insidious and dangerous foe the wireworm is calculatingly active. It will attack the roots and stems of almost every variety of garden and field plant and enjoy doing so for a period of three to five years, *see* section on PESTS.

Watch out for dry soil around the onions. Run your fingers around the bulb — go on, never mind the nail varnish, scoop away the soil and the bulb will soon become very excited and start to plump out. What with the mildew on the roses, the caking soil and all the confounded flowers running to seed, June can be a damnable month.

JULY

If you are in luck the rain could be pattering down, keeping the garden watered and you indoors. The delphiniums (dear old perennial) should be a blaze of colour that will stay with you until well into August unless (there would be an "unless") you have dry weather. In which case you had better keep watering. Although delphiniums are attractive alone you really need a mass together to appreciate the real beauty of them. Two good things about the delphinium: it is very hardy and needs no protection in the hardest winter; once planted it can remain undisturbed for at least three years.

Tie up the hollyhocks and dahlias. Too often their lower leaves are destroyed by the dreaded red spider caterpillar. A mulch of rotten manure (preferably cow manure) flung around the roots could make all the difference. Mow the lawns. Lift, divide and re-plant irises.

Keep cutting away the dead roses; remove the suckers from the roots of rose trees, otherwise they will go back to their wild state. Mulch plants with grass (lawn clippings). Cut out old fruiting canes from raspberries. Mulch vegetables. Trap slugs. Sow parsley for winter and early spring use.

Cut back parsley which is running to seed. Make up mushroom beds for the continuance of the mushroom crop. Gather and dry the herbs. Pull away loose soil from shallots to hurry up their ripening.

Start layering the strawberries. Little plantlets should have been put out by the strawberry plants. The one nearest the main plant should have its runner pushed into the ground — by you!

Keep the soil moist. When the plantlet has rooted sever it from the main plant. An alternative way to layer is to put a small pot of light soil beneath the plantlet and peg the runner into it. But I always use the former way quite successfully. When fruiting is over, set fire to the straw around the strawberries to purify the ground. Make new strawberry beds as soon as you have enough well rooted runners. Carry on trapping the jolly old slugs.

AUGUST

This is the month when the dedicated gardener could begin to reap the glorious harvest of the foresight, lavish care and hard work which he has ploughed into his garden during the previous winter, spring and even early summer. His heart may swell with justifiable pride or he may hang his head in natural despair. If the latter I would advise a good long holiday. However, if a holiday is out of the question, attend to the mildew on the roses and prune the rambler roses (not the climbers). As soon as the blooms have faded cut off all the old dark stems at ground level. If some really good new shoots are appearing on the old dark stems cut back stem to a joint which is just above the strongest new shoot. Disbud chrysanthemums. If leaves show signs of rust, spray with lime sulphur (one part to eighty of water). Renovate lawns as well as mowing them.

If you didn't do so last month peg down strawberry runners for layering. Remember strawberry plants are alleged to produce the best fruit during their first two or three years. Gather apples when ripe and wrap in oiled paper. Store apples, pears and plums in a dark frost-free area. Cut out old loganberry canes which have fruited. Bend over tops of onions. Lift and store shallots. Feed leeks with weak liquid manure. Take up the garlic, retaining some of the bulbs for planting. Sow winter and spring spinach....it is best to do this at the beginning and end of the month. Also sow winter onions and parsley in the first week of the month, unless by now you have decided to move to a high rise flat.

SEPTEMBER

The flower of the month is the dahlia. Early September plant daffodils, snowdrops, narcissi, crocuses. If you simply cannot manage it by the second week in September you would be well advised to get them in by the second week in October. Make new lawns and renovate old ones. Plant daffodils and crocuses in the lawn, if you wish. Take cuttings of roses. Lift and store gladioli. Dress soil around the blackcurrants with manure. Layer cultivated blackberries. Remove diseased leaves from strawberry plants. Prune blackcurrants, raspberries, etc. Tie up raspberries.

Lift and store onions and leeks. Lift and store beetroot, harvest turnips. Cut down mint stalks and give dressing of manure. Lift and store begonias in frost-free conditions. Plant bulbs in bowls of fibre. Cut lavender. If it will cheer you up just ignore the bit about renovating lawns. For seven years I used to consider with unhappiness doing something about my two little lawns, which I have said really look like two bits of field with their moss, buttercups, daisies and rough grass. Eventually I planted snowdrops, crocuses and daffodils, at strategic intervals under the front 'lawn' which faces due north. So, if gardening depresses you, remember it will all be here when you are long since gone.

OCTOBER

Take up, dry and then store all dahlias tubers. Divide and replant the delphiniums. They are at their most joyful in a moist situation. Sweep up leaves to rot down. Prune roses but not drastically. Replant bulbs and spring flowers.

Dress lawn for worm trouble. You can make a poisonous mixture by mixing mercuric chloride (half ounce) in one pint of boiling water and then making it up with cold water to a total solution of seven and a half gallons.

After watering the lawn you can apply the solution at the rate of one gallon to every square yard and then the worms will rise up to the surface and die. I think it very cruel. You can make a non poisonous solution by mixing freshly slaked lime with water, one ounce to the gallon. Fling this around every square yard, then collect and destroy the worms. The worms can frolic over and under my lawns as much as they like. Prick over the lawn with a fork and sprinkle old soot, well slaked lime. Do not forget that lime is a great asset to gardens but is hated by the rhododendron.

When pot plants have been reached by frost soak soil with the coldest water you can get. Sprinkle foliage with the same cold water. Put the plants in a frost-free shed and they will probably revive in a few hours. When unmistakable recovery has been made, move them into warmth. Do not cut off withered parts until a week after this treatment. Collect and save wood ash from bonfires. Turn over vacant ground and fork in manure or add lime as necessary.

When you are sweeping up the leaves remember that some leaves are harmful and should be burnt, eg. all fruit tree leaves, ash, elder, chestnut, sycamore, needles of conifer — consign them to the bonfire. The ash will come in useful. Do not try sweeping up the leaves on a day when a gale force wind is blowing. Personally,

I always hope the wind will blow all the leaves away before I get to sweep them up. But Christmas will sometimes arrive before I manage to stagger around the lawn with a broom.

Now a really useful tip. Take two pieces of wood, approximately one to one and a half feet long and one foot wide, and you will find they are really useful for moving the swept up bundles of leaves to the wheelbarrow, or in my case, plastic bag. But, believe me, leaves can be very tricky on a windy day. For leaf mould, oak and beech leaves are best. Hyacinths, daffodils, tulips and crocuses should all be planted by the third week in October. Have you made it?

NOVEMBER

If you have heavy ground give the lawn a dressing of sand, builders sand. Mulch roses with manure. Lift, dry and store montbretia bulbs in a frost-free place (I have never taken mine up!) Take cuttings of fruit bushes. Plant gooseberry bushes and redcurrant bushes. Continue to clear the ground of leaves. It is said that leaves ruin lawns so in my case there is not too much cause for alarm. Plant shallots. Manure and clear up asparagus bed.

Plant deciduous trees and shrubs while the weather remains favourable. You may get in a last cutting of the lawns if you didn't last month. But I doubt it. November is considered by many to be the beginning of the rosarian year. So plant your new roses. Suitable soil is required; not too much clay. So dig out if too much clay and put in rubbish, clinkers, ash. If it is light and sandy soil, add some clay. Bush roses should be planted at least two feet apart. November is also said to be a good time for planting fruit trees. It really is a shame that gardens can not be made in the summer by simply sitting in the shade and smiling.

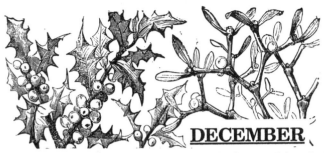

DECEMBER

If you did not do it last month prick over the lawn with a fork and brush in the builders sand. Prune fruit trees which are growing too vigorously. Remove suckers of fruit trees at their junction with the roots. Winter spray fruit trees with tar oil wash. Spray gooseberry bushes. Lime wash walls against which fruit grow. Collect and burn all vegetable refuse and apply it as a dressing to the ground — a kind of winter raiment. You can still plant fruit trees if the weather is mild. Sweep and roll the lawn. If you are really unlucky the weather could be dry enough for you to do some digging. If you leave things in the ground all winter you may lose some. So you have the choice, leave them in and cut down to within nine inches of the ground, or lift the whole plant and put in a cold frame and keep glass covering closed in periods of frost.

If the frost keeps away, outdoor chrysanthemums will continue to flower until the end of the year. If you leave them in the ground for the remainder of the winter you run the risk of losing them. As soon as they have finished flowering it would be best to shorten the stems to nine inches off the ground and transfer the whole plant to a cold frame, where fine, broken soil covered with coal ashes is best — and label them or you will not know which colour is where. Fresh green shoots should appear in the spring and can be detached and potted in sandy soil ready for replanting in the garden.

And remember, the only day that is ever wasted, is that on which you did not laugh!

INDEX

Index